First Edition.

Printed October 2015, in the United Kingdom.

Published by Spadge UK

Illustrated by Rosie Rockets | Designed by Rick Nunn | Edited by John O'Nolan

ISBN: 978-0-9934299-0-3

For Andy

Thank you for your support!
HUGE LOVE /
Spadge
X

Acknowledgements:

I highly recommend that you skip to the end of this page if you're not into heartwarmingly-offensive acceptance speeches; this book is my award and I have a lot of bellends to thank...

Thank you to all of the people I consider parents, not just for your support but for your unwavering need to feed me. Special thanks to my mum, Di, who blessed me with many genetic gifts - her humour, her warmth, her impulsive need to dance in her underwear to every Madonna song that she hears... (nobody else in Waitrose ever seems to truly appreciate this). I swear sometimes just hearing her voice gives me the answer, mostly because now she answers the phone with a simple "no." One day we will wear fleeces on national television. //Thank you to my twin sister Rosie and her girl Robyn for singing Taylor Swift songs to me whenever the going got tough. //Thanks to everyone who regularly kept me sane through my progress: Elibear, Heatherbelle, Rachums, Yazpie, Nozface, Ace Curlz, and of course my main inspiration - Andrizzle. You guys made it a lot easier. //Ash, thanks for letting me abuse you daily with every idea I ever have. You are a hero - probably one called Howdyougetinthosejeans-Man. //Thanks to the inner voice that always asks "what would Steve do?" before making a creative decision (until I chicken out and change it to something more law-abiding). Bennys for life. //Thank you John, for always pushing me to think bigger and for talking me into printing a period joke, somehow. I owe you so much. //And a ridiculously big thank you to my better half, Rick; a man with more patience than I thought humanly possible. I'm sorry for accusing you of domestic abuse every time you didn't let me eat your half of the pizza. Words are my life, and yours mean more to me than any others.

Most importantly - thank you, the Maverick reading this right now. Life is full of what I call 'Big Mac Moments'. You purchase a Big Mac, expecting there to be a beautiful twin-tiered burger inside. What you actually reveal is something that looks (and smells) like a hedgehog that's suffocated itself in a web of plastic cheese. I still eat them once a week... but my point is that I hope this book isn't that kind of experience for you.

Thank you for taking this chance on me.

The title:

Being braver than Britain is quite a statement to make, I know. I once watched a man eat a yogurt a whole month past its sell-by date. But statistically, this book is evidence that in less than a year, I beat Britain's top 10 biggest fears.

To make this mission even slightly impressive, you probably need to know what those fears are. Don't worry, we'll get to that. Whenever I've mentioned this project to anyone, I've always asked them to guess what they think the top 10 biggest fears are and, if that has taught me anything; it's that you should put aside your own assumptions.

Fear is insanely erratic and differs greatly between people. If I had a fear of pens, for example, most people wouldn't recognise what a huge achievement stepping into a stationary shop would be for me! Similarly, if these fears consisted of being eaten alive by wild animals, or trapping my hand in a letter box and having to drag a door around for the rest of my life, then I'd probably have to give up on this idea and find another hobby.

Luckily for me, the chances of completing this mission with all limbs intact is pretty high. They say fortune favours the brave. Otherwise, please expect a slight delay when I have to type out the rest of this story with my face.

THE AUTHOR:

It's also worth throwing my 'tendency to be pathetic' into the mix. You may not be fully aware of just how much of a wimp I am. A large majority of my family (my fat brother) isn't even remotely impressed that I'm attempting this. He doesn't find a single thing on the list intimidating. This upsetting fact is probably some kind of genius scientific breakthrough (that fear isn't something genetic) but enough about these humanity-changing discoveries, I'm here to prove that I can actually do this. And that, unimpressed reader, will be some kind of miracle.

On the courageous scale I'm somewhere between 'dangerously prone to panic attack' and 'just play dead'. I've lived in Britain my whole life and those 27 years have brought me face-to-face with a large amount of British people, and (probably unrelated) frequent sensations of irrational fear.

Seriously, I'm panicking most of the time, even when I'm asleep or having a casual discussion with the Sainsbury's delivery man about the sheer diversity of potatoes. Of these hundreds or even thousands of people that I have met, if I was asked at random: "would you consider yourself braver than the person next to you?" I would confidently and ever so eloquently answer "Hell no." Even if that person was a crying 6 year old. Or 2 year old. I probably shouldn't curse.

I also love my grandma, a lot, but if she needed rescuing from a smaller than average house-spider in her bathroom, then her fate would rest entirely on the accuracy of my shoe-throwing skills. In which personal experience has taught me that two shoes are rarely enough. I now carry a third in my handbag for such emergencies.

My point is, nobody would expect me to hold the title 'Braver than Britain'. And that's just the kind of motivation I need.

THE IDEA:

The average British spider isn't going to hurt anyone; it's lighter than most feathers (is that part of what makes them scary though, like gravity-defying ninjas?). Some humans (ones I will never understand) even keep them as pets. So why do other people hate them so much? If there was a lion in the bathroom then I'd understand the logic behind the physical reaction of soiling myself, but I happen to have (sensibly) chosen a lifestyle that requires very little interaction with lions on a daily basis.

Similarly, if I happened to be in South America (home to the most deadly spider in the world) then finding one in the bathroom could easily ruin my day but, here in the UK, surely our instincts are slightly off target? I decided to do the research — where does this fear of spiders sit on the 'most feared' list?...

The List:

Britain's top 10 fears:
According to a 2014 survey by YouGov.

Acrophobia	-	*Fear of heights*
Ophidiophobia	-	*Fear of snakes*
Glossophobia	-	*Fear of public speaking*
Arachnophobia	-	*Fear of spiders*
Claustrophobia	-	*Fear of small spaces*
Musophobia	-	*Fear of mice*
Trypanophobia	-	*Fear of needles*
Pteromerhanophobia	-	*Fear of flying*
Agoraphobia	-	*Fear of crowds*
Coulrophobia	-	*Fear of clowns*

Spiders are fourth. Interesting.

My first thought was that some of the phobias on that list don't seem so bad! It was this small moment of false security that started it all…

The beginning:

Brain: "Hey Body, why don't you try to conquer that entire list?"

Body: "...."

Because bodies can't speak, Shakira, despite what you sing about.

Game on, Brain. Count me in.

Statistically, it is very unlikely that a single person would suffer from all 10 phobias. Some of them I would even enjoy (mice and snakes = cute/slithery, respectively) but many of them are very rational things to fear. Heights could lead to falling, flying could lead to crashing, and you only have to watch Saw (2004) to realise that clowns are often hiding a mentally-unstable murderous-streak.

Now I'm inviting you to follow me into my 10-month journey of fear conquering. Would you have ever selected me as your leader? In a very restricted situation I'd like to think that you might. Where do I start? As with everything in life, probably with the easy ones. Will I actually fly for the first time in over a decade (my biggest fear)? The thought of it makes my insides leak.

Are you ready? Let's go make Grandma proud.

Chapters:

Fears listed from least to most common.

Chapter One:

Fear 10 - Coulrophobia

(fear of clowns)

Coulrophobia:

What it is: **Clowns**
How rational I think it is: **1/5**
How much I fear it: **0/5**
The date I faced it: **30th July 2015**
How I conquered it: **Gleefully**

Rational scale:
0 = irrational, 1 = not very, 2 = relatively, 3 = reasonably, 4 = rational, 5 = very rational

Fear scale:
0 = happy, 1 = easy, 2 = ambivalent, 3 = dislike, 4 = hate, 5 = need new pants

The Phobia:

Of the country's ten greatest fears, the people of Britain have chosen clowns as the least terrifying. Looking at this list, I think I'd probably agree with that. Clowns are usually regular human beings, wearing a costume; a (respected) professional that ten year olds tend to bully at birthday parties. They are, for the most part, normal, everyday people.

Do I dislike them? Sure. I feel the same way about anyone who is paid to be annoyingly happy (e.g. Subway staff) but to be scared of someone who couldn't possibly outrun me in those huge shoes? Nah.

When did this enjoyable clown experience start turning into a nightmare?

Is it due to the bad reputation clowns have been given by the 'horror' film industry? You know, the kind of movie where they murder people or rob banks. *It* and *The Dark Knight* are classic movie examples that depict clowns as sewer-trolling, money-stealing, child-catching, murderers. We sure could use a Batman right now.

Despite movies and television recently projecting this

image of evil clowns onto our frontal lobes, coulrophobia is not a new phobia at all. The demise of the entertainer-clown started well over 200 years ago. As far back as 1849, there have been stories of vindictive jesters seeking revenge. *Hop-Frog* by Edgar Allen Poe, for example, tells the story of a deformed jester convincing people to dress as orangutans covered in tar; before setting them all on fire. Brutal.

General clowns though, were around centuries before that. There was a type of clown in ancient Rome called the Stupidus and as early as 2500 BCE, pygmy clowns were making pharaohs laugh in ancient Egypt. Clowns had one job; to entertain by projecting fun and humour, which was often dosed with lots of alcohol, impressions and slapstick comedy. Alcohol often meant that clowns lacked judgement, didn't live long, and frequently suffered long-term side effects such as depression.

Perhaps, logically, the scariest thing about clowns is the fact that they hide their identity with makeup and emphasised dysmorphic features. I was once scared of Santa because of the huge beard and glasses as a child, for the same reasons. I now feel the same way about hipsters. Clowns hide their faces with makeup and their natural hair with a wig, they surprise you with tricks which seem out of the ordinary (or a swift pie to the face) and I can see how that would put many people on edge.

Why do clowns hide their identity though, or at least alter it? If making people laugh was your job, wouldn't you want to be recognised for it? It is said that a clown's makeup began with rosy cheeks; helping those individuals to project an image of being drunk and merry (and less hungover) to the audience. One of the first well-known, brightly-coloured clowns was a man called Joseph Grimaldi, who performed in the early 1800's. His story is actually quite depressing, but I feel it adds to the creepiness of the 'jolly' costume. Grimaldi's life was full of misery and misfortune; he lost many of his loved ones to premature deaths (one in childbirth and another to alcohol). So during his acts he would perform elaborate, violent slapstick, that caused him pain and deformities for the rest of his life. When a young Charles Dickens wrote a book about Grimaldi's life, he described this self-torture beautifully; for every laugh he wrought from his audiences, Grimaldi suffered commensurate pain. It seems there is a dark side to being a clown, one that is easily covered with bright colours and makeup.

It's very much common sense to fear a human who is hiding their identity. I feel it begs the question "what else are they hiding?" People are more likely to get up to no good if they can't be identified. This thought often crosses my mind when people ask me "what's the best part about being an identical twin?" The ability to murder. Obviously.

When I was young, I remember fondly seeing a clown and feeling nothing but joy. I was once greeted by Ronald McDonald in a McDonalds restaurant when I was about seven years old. He was giving out boxes of chicken nuggets and Disney toys. That kind of positive influence is probably what you need to overcome a fear like this. I imagine that if airplane staff had given me tasty chicken-treats and toys when I was young, I'd probably love those fart-filled death traps now, too.

Maybe.

Thinking about it, a clown would be a great job for me. Not because I'm secretly depressed, but because I'd literally be getting paid to throw pies in children's faces. Seriously though, impressing kids is hard; they've all seen 'Extreme Balloon Animal-ing' videos on YouTube, where some energy drink company has sponsored sports-stars to make balloon animals while cliff diving. So, watching an overweight person 'make' a balloon snake, while dressed in an ugly outfit that distinctly lacks a parachute, is unlikely to impress anyone.

Being unimpressed by a clown would not have gone down well in the Middle Ages. If you didn't make the king laugh then he would have your face mutilated into a constant smile; cutting the muscles that allowed you to frown. I can see why a constantly smiling face would be kind of creepy, as well as very impractical; imagine complaining about your meal at a restaurant or attending a funeral in that state...

Perhaps I'll give this job a miss after all. I'll just throw pies at kids from the bus window, as usual.

How am I even going to do this? A lot of these challenges will require very little planning-effort on my part. The majority of them (flying, needles, snakes) will just require showing up and sitting down/waiting for certain death. This one, however, will need to be arranged because I don't come across many clowns in my day-to-day life, especially scary ones. Halloween only comes around once a year (very much like the dreaded hipster-Santa) and even then, there simply aren't enough of them.

I feel that setting up this challenge will be a mission in itself. What a tricky way to start. Wish me luck!

MY CHALLENGE:

As predicted, real-life clowns are legitimately extinct. I couldn't even find one relatively locally, never mind a circus-full! According to *TheAtlantic.com*, a group called Clown International has lost almost 90 percent of its members since its peak in the 1980s and those numbers continue to decrease. Children just don't like clowns anymore.

Still, I decided to email one that I found on Facebook; a professional, asking if I could just hang out with him for a day. Let's just say he "politely declined" It's possible I came on a little strong/mental. Perhaps I was just a little too old for him.

I tried to go scarier (clown-wise, not stalker-wise), creating the scariest scenario that I could think of; something like 'Night of the Horror Clown III'. Confronting a bunch of freaky-looking people with terrifying agendas. Much like my first Fresher's Week.

There are two problems with this idea though — 1. I don't have many friends willing to buy an entire clown outfit for a project that doesn't really benefit them 2. I don't have many friends close-by.

I decided that it was a good idea to ask people with coulrophobia what they think it is that terrifies them specifically.
The most popular response was their "scary faces" — their
frozen smiles and lack of emotion - the way their makeup
or mask hides their facial features. So I needed to hide a lot
of faces for this challenge. "Hey man, not spoken to you in
ages, do you mind if I dress you up in a ridiculous costume
for a photo in a random alleyway?" My friends are super
lucky. Maybe that's why they all moved so far away...

I set myself a £100 budget and bought as many different
clown masks from eBay as I could find. The scarier the
better. I spent exactly £66.60 on masks, which is pretty
creepy in itself. Now I just needed people to fill them. I had
13 masks but if I could get more clowns than I have fingers
(I have ten of those, despite being forced to use cutlery on
a regular basis), I'll be happy.

Some people declined my invite, not just because I get
weirdly sexual when asking people for favours, but because
they have a huge fear of clowns; so much so that they can't
even look at the masks! Amazing for my overall feeling of
accomplishment, but not overly helpful in getting my numbers up. I managed to blackmail a few others with cookies
and the promise of a small amount of fame within these
pages. Plus, I let them keep the masks afterwards because
some of them are definitely into weird stuff.

The 13 masks were absolutely horrifying; some had missing eyes and jaws, and I had somehow managed to talk 13
people into meeting me in a specific location at the same
time. What made this challenge slightly more daunting
was that I didn't know some of the people that would be

showing up (friends of friends, etc. although I guess nothing helps you bond like being creeped out by a stranger wearing a clown mask). Once the masks were on, it would be increasingly difficult to tell who was who, which I think adds to the terror of it all. "Which one of you is chasing me/touching my ass?"

As we travelled to the creepy location with a box full of masks on my lap, I started to feel a little bit nervous for the first time. My destination of choice was underneath an old bridge by a local railway line, and I asked everyone to arrive dressed in dark colours. The idea was to make the white masks stand out more against the black background.

Once I knew everyone was there, I left the area so that people could get ready. As I waited, alone by a bridge bypass, I swear the air seemed to get colder and heavier. I started to miss having company. When I returned, I was met by this thug-like group of terrifying weirdos (no offence, friends and colleagues) who were moving around in intimidating positions, tilting their heads to one side and crawling towards me. With these newly-grotesque and unfamiliar faces looking directly at me, I felt very uncomfortable and intimidated. It was nowhere near as easy as I thought it would be to approach them. I had to remind myself that these were real 'safe' people, who had apparently been hiding very convincing vigilante mannerisms for years.

Members of the public occasionally had to walk past this scene that we had created, and it was hilarious to witness their shocked reactions. Some of them looked intrigued too, but most seemed to be thinking more along the lines of "please don't mug me" and I realised that as a group, we could have easily been out to rob a bank. "Where were you at 8:30pm on Thursday?" "Well, Officer, I was lurking under a bridge wearing a clown mask and black hoody…"

I needed some photos to show that I had actually immersed myself within these clowns ("It's nice to meet you, friend of a friend, can you get so that I can feel your breath on my neck, please?"). We set up a couple of scenes. I want you to know that the look on my face is genuine. For one of the pictures everyone screamed at me just before the shutter-button was pressed, creating some extra tension (and potential 999 calls).

This was such a stressful challenge to organise; it took a lot of preparation, but I think the hard work paid off. The whole thing was a lot more scary than I thought it would be, especially as it got darker outside and their masked-faces appeared to be suspended in nothingness. It was the stuff nightmares are made of.

I have a lot more sympathy for coulrophobics now, but it was still quite a fun challenge to complete.

I just want to say thank you so much to all of my wonderful clowns for your spontaneous acting skills. That was the best thing about this by far; getting to share it with so many awesome people.

Other things I did that qualify conquering clowns:

It's been an almost upsettingly clown-free year, but I did go into McDonalds an awful lot. In the hope of an encounter, of course. So, you know – at least I tried hard. I also went to bed with full make-up on after a night out and woke up resembling The Joker.

Chapter Two:

FEAR 9 – AGORAPHOBIA

(fear of crowds)

Agoraphobia:

What it is: **Crowds**
How rational I think it is: **4/5**
How much I fear it: **4/5**
The date I faced it: **28th August 2015**
How I conquered it: **Reluctantly**

Rational scale:
0 = irrational, 1 = not very, 2 = relatively, 3 = reasonably, 4 = rational, 5 = very rational

Fear scale:
0 = happy, 1 = easy, 2 = ambivalent, 3 = dislike, 4 = hate, 5 = need new pants

THE PHOBIA:

Crowds are horrible things. They're basically a mass of body heat (and therefore bodily fluids) blocking you from where you want to go or slowing you down. Lack of personal space and, in many cases, pleasant smells is just uncomfortable. You feel hot, stressed and you're bound to catch something. It's a good, logical fear to have: 'Avoid an infestation of other human beings at all costs, for your own safety and wellbeing'. They should put that sign in tube stations.

But where does this phobia come from? A fear of crowds can develop for numerous reasons. When you're in a crowd there's more competition for all of the things which generally keep us in good health; like food, oxygen and enough space to move around freely. Being inside a crowd can also affect your ability to hear and see anything else that is around you; two senses that are generally regarded as fundamental to human survival. A mass crowd is a potential for mass chaos.

Not only does being surrounded obstruct your exit-strategy in all directions, but these 'objects' that are blocking you in also have the gift of consciousness. Any embarrassment caused on your part wouldn't go unnoticed. I once almost vomited whilst trapped in a crowd, which wouldn't have been pleasant for anybody involved.

Agoraphobia is a bit like a dirty combination of public speaking and claustrophobia, which arguably makes it worse than both of those things. Yet here it sits at number nine on your list, unexpectedly low on the scale. I'm surprised, Britain. I'm also very reluctant to put myself in another so-stressed-that-I-am-close-to-puking situation.

I put a lot of effort into avoiding large groups of people, usually. Especially when attempting tasks such as trying to find the most perfectly ripe avocado in M&S (that might sound fancy, but they're under a pound and you get the bonus of University-Challenge-levels of banter at the checkout for free). Things can get pretty feisty when there are a lot of hands in the avocado crate all at once. As a general rule, I try to stick to off-peak times when visiting shops. Otherwise I bail and hide my full basket in one of the freezers, returning when I don't have to fake-sneeze my way to the front of the shelves or simply settle for what I can reach. Looks like it's a dinner of broccoli, sour cream and use-by-today egg mayo. Again.

The main problem with busy places is that other people are annoying. They're slow and/or loud, block the aisles and touch each other inappropriately – or worse – touch the ripest avocado that I had my eye on.

My friends love shopping on a Saturday, for example, but you can't reach the clothes without banging your shin on one of the baby-buggies that has been parked unceremoniously between your current location and that amazing emoji jumper. The Starbucks coffee always tastes more burnt when lines are full, the newsagents have sold out of papers and by 1pm all of the size 5 shoes have gone.

Damn my perfectly average foot-size.

A bad queue is still better than a good crowd though; queues leave you with an escape route either side, crowds are like a 360-degree queue of doom that never moves. A quick exit is impossible from a crowd. You either have to squeeze through the bodies like jelly through a straw or try the old 'bulldozer method' which (from experience) often leads to a nose bleed. No bleeding on the new size 4 shoes, people; I need to return them for being too small.

Let's hope this challenge is shorter than the Primark queue.

MY CHALLENGE:

For me, being trapped in a crowd is a lot worse than being trapped in a small space. Now, I would need to subject myself to one of epic proportions.

Despite boldly facing crowded situations multiple times a week – like restaurants, cinemas, and any street during rush hour – I tried to think of a horrible situation that I'd never been in before.

I'm not a fan of being pushed around in a mosh pit, but I've done that many, many times. Plus, the space-restrictions of the venue mean that crowds can only grow so big. I needed a bigger crowd; I needed an open space with a lot more people.

It just so happened to be festival season as I sat quietly pondering this conundrum. I'd never been remotely tempted to go to a festival before, not just because of my crowd-hatred, but also because I have a minor existential crisis every time it's suggested that paying £15 for a burger (and pooping in a mud-hole) might be a pleasurable experience. This felt like the perfect opportunity to finally tackle this unhygienic nightmare.

I foolishly trusted my friend Tom when he proposed a trip to Leeds Festival. Tom, as it turns out, has a rather cunning tendency to disguise PURE EVIL as helpfulness. I checked out some of the line-ups and bought a couple of tickets. I chose a day ticket for the Friday, hoping that traffic would be better than the weekend tickets. £144 well spent for a good few hours of self-inflicted torture. Excitement failed me, but at least I'd get a wristband and could pretend to be cool for a while.

Leeds Festival is the 2nd biggest music festival in the UK, second only to Glastonbury which had an attendance in 2015 of 153,000 people. I really was surprised at how many people attend these things, because when you think about it, that is a lot of poo.

The line-up looked pretty good; The Libertines, The Maccabees and The Gaslight Anthem (all the 'the's) but after speaking to previous Leeds Festival attendees, I soon discovered that the experience might be occasionally tainted by a flying bottle of piss. Who does that? The same goes for people who destroy things during the performances; starting fires and acting like general idiots. I was in for a treat.

It turned out that I hadn't made this challenge easy for myself (and I hated Tom a little bit more), although I guess 'easy' defeats the entire point of this project. Perhaps it was for the best (Tom was allowed to keep one of his arms).

When I next saw Tom I asked him:

"Have you ever been to Leeds Fest before, Tommo?"

and so came the unquestionably timeless response:

"Ah mate, not since Date-rape Dave piped one out down the side of a tent."

My excitement level remained at sub-zero.

With one eye on my calendar and the other on the weather, I prayed for dry spells. I imagined that the only thing more depressing than standing in a field, surrounded by neon-covered teenagers, would be doing the same thing in a very wet field. Luck seemed to be unexpectedly on my side and the weather predicted a sunny 21 degrees. Not that a prediction ever helps us out much in the UK.

I packed sunscreen, a raincoat and enough hand sanitiser to sterilise a small farm, or indeed, a sexual predator.

Nothing dampens the spirit of adventure more quickly than a queue of traffic as far as the eye can see. The stiff-neck was setting in quickly as I pondered how something so mundane could destroy your hopes and dreams, while simultaneously testing the physical limits of your bladder. My determination wavered with every sat-nav update. Rick and I weren't even half way to Leeds at this point. He had to bribe me back into the car by rubbing Nutella into his beard at the service station; I could see the queue of traffic from the car park. We arrived almost two hours later than planned (and with Rick covered in ants).

Set in the grounds of Bramham Park near Wetherby, the track to the Leeds Fest car park had clearly been designed in preparation for queuing traffic; it wound for miles through a bumpy woodland track. We must have timed it well, because it seemed to take forever to see any other cars. Even with all the windows down we couldn't hear any kind of music. If it wasn't for the hippy-attendants pointing unenthusiastically in alternating directions, I would have questioned being in the right place at all.

Once we'd located a field that resembled a car park, or rather a car park that once resembled a field, we put on our wellies and trudged grumpily to find the entrance. For TWO MILES, we clomped past people dragging tents and sacks of alcohol over a very bumpy track. Teenage girls were talking loudly about how much they loved having breasts now (ahh, to be 18 again) and guys with fluorescent-white teeth were taking it in turns to wrestle each other into the mud.

The entrance induced a small twinge of excitement for the first time, as I tried not to think about how far away the car now was. It wouldn't be a quick escape if I suddenly felt like I needed to get out, but it was as least time for the sacred wristband to be attached. Another small piece of evidence that I had kicked fear's ass once more.

Inside, was mayhem. A sea of tents lined the horizon as far as the eye could see. There was litter everywhere, a strong smell of noodles and brightly-lit fairground rides released the occasional screaming sound into the sky.

There was a clear pathway between the tents full of sunburnt people and impressive looking food-trucks, and so we made our way in that direction. There was fresh stone-baked pizza, flavoured noodles, churros and dips, and lots of alcohol. You're forced to walk along a path of overpriced items; waterproof clothes, hats, sunglasses, those flower headbands that everyone seems to wear, wellies and neon paint. It seemed that retailers had caught on quickly to what's in demand in places like this. Did I mention there was lots of alcohol?

As we reached the edge of the campsite, I noticed that a lot more people had caught up with us. For the first time I caught a real glimpse of the crowd. The daily capacity of Leeds Fest is 90,000, and I had just reached the 'feel-me-down' security checkpoint to join them. Through this gate was a collection of 5 stages, each with varying performances from well-known artists. I had one mission; to get to the main stage and stand in the biggest crowd we could find.

This was by far the busiest place I'd ever been to. People were already being carried out by their limbs, passed-out drunk, or laid across the floor and being stepped over. There were people with babies strapped onto their backs and people dancing to the weirdest music I'd ever heard. Chaos in every direction. I found it hard to focus on anything; I was constantly distracted by gangs of people bursting into song or Snapchatting their friends. Short-shorts and Hunter wellies seemed to be the trend, regardless of gender, and I felt very uncool (if not very clean) compared to the majority of the people there.

Stepping over people, pizza and other matter that probably used to be food, we made it to the main stage. Every instinct told me to avoid entering this crowd, but Rick kept pushing through. Halfway into the crowd, we hit a huge metal barrier that ran the length of the stage. We were already surrounded by people in every direction but Rick shouted (the music was very loud at this point) "We can get closer!" I didn't have the energy or the vocal-projection to argue, so I followed about seven paces behind.

We found the busiest area we could get to, but once we stopped walking. I was hit with exhaustion and started to feel a bit faint. We hadn't stopped walking at mission-speed the entire time and I wasn't breathing properly. I didn't feel well at all. Rick – supportive as ever – ordered me to stand as close to strangers as I could and held the GoPro up above my head. This, unsurprisingly, drew a lot of unwanted attention as I instantly started to feel worse. "GoPro bas-tards!" shouted a group of guys from behind us and I just wanted the ground to swallow me up. Rick has no problem with that kind of attention: "Who cares? We'll never see them again" he shouted in my general direction, but I was pretty close to tears with my discomfort.

I barely even noticed that The Maccabees were on stage, my eyes were constantly scanning the sheer amount of people around us. We stayed in that spot for about the length of one song, then I needed to get out. Just get to an edge of some kind. With oxygen.

Once we reached the edge and the camera was stowed once more, I felt a lot better. Like I was over the hardest part of a mountain climb and I could see the other side. I needed sugar to stop myself from shaking. I couldn't believe that people do this for fun; staying in this crowded field for days at a time, laughing, singing and exchanging STIs like Pokémon.

After a selection of refreshments and a few feeble attempts to take in some of the slightly less intimidating areas of the festival, we began the long walk back to the car. As we made it to the end of the campsite, we turned around to take in one last view and watched the sun set over the huge array of brightly coloured tents. The air started to get chillier and my feet started to ache. We had walked more than five miles with only a few minutes of rest.

As we reached the exit by the car park, the security guy said "Day tickets? Once you're out you're out!" and we couldn't have smiled more. "Yep." (the happiest of all 'yes's.) Goodbye Leeds Fest, I hope I don't have to stand in a crowd that big again for a long, long time.

Other things I did that qualify conquering crowds:

Crowds are difficult to escape when you live in a city. On a weekly basis I encountered crowds at cinemas, restaurants, train stations, business events, brothels...

Chapter Three:

Fear 8 – Pteromerhanophobia

(fear of flying)

Pteromerhanophobia:

What it is: **Flying**
How rational I think it is: **5/5**
How much I fear it: **6/5**
The date I faced it: **14th May 2015**
How I conquered it: **Hatefully**

Rational scale:
0 = irrational, 1 = not very, 2 = relatively, 3 = reasonably, 4 = rational, 5 = very rational

Fear scale:
0 = happy, 1 = easy, 2 = ambivalent, 3 = dislike, 4 = hate, 5 = need new pants

The Phobia:

Time to get serious. There are many things in life that I find hard to believe. Aliens, gravity, people who eat half a Mars bar and save the rest for later. But how the Hell 'flying' didn't come at the very top of the phobia list, I'll never understand.

Not only will this challenge be the hardest for me to complete (mentally), it is also the hardest to accurately put 'how extreme my fear is' into words. You honestly couldn't ask me to do anything worse (with the exception of jumping out of the plane, maybe). I came very close to crying during my last flight, I remember it well, and that was almost 12 years ago now.

My main issue with trying to conquer this fear is that it's not a quick one to get over with. I have to book and plan this in advance and that leaves me with more time to chicken out; something I am renowned for doing. There's pressure to be on that exact flight, at that exact time, and I even have to check-in two hours before the takeoff. That's two hours of sitting in an airport, trying not to think about flying. Absolutely impossible.

I did consider trying a local airfield and doing a short flight around the county, but I felt that wouldn't be throwing myself into a real experience. I'd kick myself for making it too easy and not having to deal with the same problems that most people dread with this phobia.

There is a great story about the brothers who were the first people to successfully invent the airplane; The Wright Brothers. In the early 1900s, there was a great amount of competition to create the world's first 'Flying Machine'. One of their competitors; a guy called Samuel Pierpont Langley, had a limitless budget, he held a seat at Harvard and was very well connected. He hired the best minds money could find and the market conditions were ideal. The New York times followed him everywhere and everybody was waiting for his success. The Wright Brothers were in a much more limited position; they worked using the income from their bicycle shop and hired people with a simple passion for machines – not a single person on their team had a college education, including the brothers. The difference was that The Wright Brothers worked for a cause rather than profit. They wanted to change the course of the world, and they were successful in doing so. On the day they first flew their flying machine in 1903, Samuel Pierpont Langley quit, rather than work to improve their design. I love a good underdog success story.

Flying is a phobia that psychologists say genuinely takes more effort than most to overcome, this is because it's not just a single fear that causes the phobia. Let's break down this fear-concoction that is otherwise known as 'flying':

1. Heights. Oh, you noticed that the ground was thousands of feet below, huh? Probably the highest height you'll ever reach.

2. Small spaces. Not much of the old leg-room.

3. Crowds. Even if you're on a plane with the nicest people, there's a lot of them packed tightly into one space. A lot of strangers and then twice the eyeballs.

4. Drunk people. Planes serve alcohol on-board. Great, that's what we want; liquid that makes people pee/puke more while on a vehicle with limited toilets.

5. Being trapped. It's hard to step outside for some air.

6. Becoming travel sick. Altitude/turbulence/turning is not fun.

7. Witnessing panic attacks/illness. Seeing it often causes a ripple effect.

8. Lack of control. You're not allowed to drive yourself. You're not even allowed to speak to the pilot, that's ultimate lack of control.

9. Long durations. Commonly, flights are not as short as car journeys in the UK.

10. Other vehicles (cars, for example) are renowned for breaking down. If that happens to a plane while you're on-board – fiery death.

Mix all of these things into one single ballache of a challenge, and you quite literally have created a real-life nightmare in one aluminium-wrapped package. I may as well just fill the plane with spiders and get it over with (Note to self: Call Samuel about Spiders on a Glider idea).

I see people in the airport struggling with their luggage, literally having to drive it around on forklifts, and I'm thinking "that weight is about to be added to a flight that is already full of people?" How do planes take off? Logic goes straight out of the window. Take the 80 tons of metal (for the average Boeing 737) then add the luggage (heavy enough to require wheels) and the 189 passengers (statistically almost definitely overweight). Are we completely sure that this is going to remain in the air?

You know what else is annoying; people who say "it's the safest way to travel!" Because they are actually right. Flying has a 99% travel-success rate. I blame the media for allowing us think otherwise. The news seems to fixate on plane crashes because on the rare occasion one crashes, a large number of people die at once. The news has completely blown up (shouldn't say "blown up") the scare factor. For weeks you'll hear about it on the radio, see the story on the TV and read about it in headlines, constantly. It puts the worst associations in our minds and skews our senses; plane = death. That association hits me hard. In my mind I'm like "avoid planes, avoid death" – it really is that simple.

In the rare instance where getting on a plane is ABSO-LUTELY ESSENTIAL then I want to be sat in an inflatable raft, on my own, wearing a parachute, holding a flare gun in each hand, while also being heavily sedated. And, if I land safely, I'll then be reduced to spending the entire trip worrying about the flight back.

I don't wanna.

But, damn it, I'm gonna.

MY CHALLENGE:

I honestly wasn't sure that I'd do this. So much so, that I only booked a one-way flight, genius I know... I didn't think about getting back home afterwards. Just kidding, I booked a train back from Edinburgh (under the assumption that I would survive the flight out, of course).

I hated every single nano-second of planning this challenge. Even just the flight confirmation email made me gag and the airport experience provoked a hive-type rash that started climbing up the sides of my neck.

I don't know if you've ever been to East Midlands Airport, but it's very small in comparison to most popular ones in Britain. This fact filled me with false hope that it wouldn't be too crowded. Wrong, Spadge, so wrong. Get in the sea.

The first part of the airport was quite pleasant. We walked straight up to the check-in desk and scanned our ticket barcodes without delay. No queue. No 'wrong way round' to scan your ticket. No worries. Done. Next, you had to kind of meander your way through retail land-mines (which is not so easy with a huge backpack) with minimal produce-damage. Level completed. Next came the boss-level of Mission Airport; the security check.

The queues were endless and the people in them were hideous. They were drunk, throwing shoes at each other and wearing matching dresses (which, I'm pretty sure, had the number of men they'd forced into bed emblazoned on the back). I stood in silence, praying that the queue would move quickly, although I wasn't at all excited about the prospect of getting closer to the plane on the other side of it either.

Something you should know about me is that I am never ill-prepared for anything, but nobody told me about the 100ml liquid rule. As someone who hasn't been to an airport (while wearing a big-girl bra) in a long time, all I knew about them had been learned from Netflix; don't forget your passport and smuggle all drugs internally.

My backpack was packed to perfection; it was like a beautiful game of Tetris in there. Carry-on luggage was all I had and now I had to throw a good 20% of it away. The 20% that was dotted around in six different backpack compartments, apparently. Some items were brand new and I almost sobbed as I unpacked it all, while also showing the hen-do parties how to fold their socks into their bra-cups to save space. You're welcome, Denise '49 and counting' Smith.

This level was rounded-off nicely with a horrible security man screaming "shoes!!!!!" at me as I approached him. I thought I was going to be tackled to the floor. Despite the array of dodgy-looking individuals queuing around me, it seemed that I was the only one who looked like she was smuggling flick-knives in her boots. I started to reconsider the power of my 'confident walk' – as well as whether I really wanted to go through with this.

As we waited in the lounge/bar/restaurant/plane-watch-ing-station, I popped 2 travel tablets and sat up-wind of Rick while he devoured a huge Burger King. The waiting was only slightly more pleasant than the queuing, so I passed the time by being glued to the screen that announc-es gate numbers. I just wanted to get on the plane and get it over with. The hives had spread all the way down to my ankles and I wanted to roll around in milk. To occupy my mind, I wrote a list of all the 110ml+ liquids I had to replace once we landed. I was surprised my that pen hadn't been confiscated as a weapon.

After what seemed like decades of stress-peeing, the board finally updated and we made our way to the gate. Death-gate. The plane looked much smaller than I expected (it held about 100 people), yet we all kept filtering through the door like sheep to the slaughter. I couldn't help but think as my foot left the ground "I hope this isn't the last piece of floor I ever stand on."

I was somewhat distracted from that cheery thought by a very enthusiastic member of the cabin crew on the warm side of the plane door. "These wee men take forever to remove their jackets before they sit down, dear. They don't care how cold you are." She was also unintentionally my new best friend. Her jokes somehow helped me breathe, and to this day she won't know how grateful I am for her presence on this flight.

The plane was set out in two rows of two, with an aisle built for ants down the middle. My claustrophobia was already kicking my ass, hard, and I hadn't even fastened my seatbelt yet. I tried to count the positives: I couldn't see any drunks, children or drunk children. So that was a good start. The air vents above our seats were blowing out cold air and I couldn't see any snakes — I didn't really have much to complain about at all. And I really love complaining.

Before I knew it, the engine was roaring and we were moving forwards, slowly at first and then much faster. Rick offered his hand to me in support and I was sad to find no Diazepam in there. I squeezed it appreciatively all the same and tried to smile.

The young business man and woman in the seats in front of us had become well acquainted and I was enjoying listening to their flirty conversation, when I was suddenly interrupted by the horrible pull of my stomach. The aircraft had left the ground. I daren't look out of the window but closing my eyes made me feel worse, so I just stared ahead and wished the time away. The climb seemed to take forever, not helped by the fact that I was fighting the urge to throw up. The small plane seemed to move continuously up and down as it turned onto its course, and I couldn't help but notice the ground appear (very, very far below) out of the left-side windows. How was everyone else so calm at this point?

The flight, in total, was just over an hour (bearing in mind that an hour is a long time when you're panicking) and after 20 minutes the plane seemed to find its ideal height and direction. I started to feel a little better; my nausea had shifted into the 'mild' category, hindered somewhat by the gropey-conversation of the people in front. I'm still scarred by their tedious innuendos to be honest, more-so than by the Pteromerhanophobia...

Once the plane had stopped surprising us with random altitude tests, the whole flight seemed much more bearable. I even plucked up the courage to peer out of the window a couple of times (before retreating back into the depths of my seat).

I watched the fasten-seatbelt sign as if I was going to win a prize when it lit up, and it didn't disappoint. Going down was much more gradual than going up and I enjoyed seeing the ground get closer.

It was almost over and I was so close to being able to finally relax. I could look forward to eating for the first time that day and, most importantly, once we landed I could finally ask out the flight attendant without throwing up on her. (She laughed at that a lot more than Rick did.)

While conquering this challenge, I still had 5 others left to complete but, as the plane touched the ground again, I knew that nothing else could possibly be this difficult for me. At about 20,000 feet in the air, I had reached the hardest point of this entire project. It felt so good to be back on solid ground.

I am so very proud of myself for this. And you know what? The beauty of Edinburgh was almost, almost worth the trauma. Almost.

Other things I did that qualify conquering flying:

I avoided flying at all costs, but I was prescribed some new migraine medication which gave me the same feeling, just in the comfort of my own living room... floor.

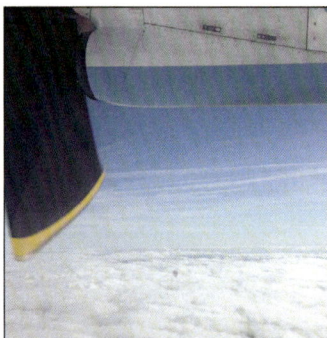

Chapter Four:

Fear 7 - Trypanophobia

(fear of needles)

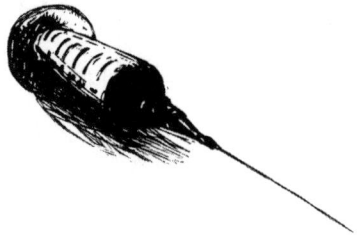

Trypanophobia:

What it is: **Needles**
How rational I think it is: **3/5**
How much I fear it: **1/5**
The date I faced it: **22nd June 2015**
How I conquered it: **Graciously**

Rational scale:
0 = irrational, 1 = not very, 2 = relatively, 3 = reasonably, 4 = rational, 5 = very rational

Fear scale:
0 = happy, 1 = easy, 2 = ambivalent, 3 = dislike, 4 = hate, 5 = need new pants

The Phobia:

"Spadge is no stranger to the needle" announces my mother to the guests at one of her many charity brunches.

She's not wrong but, to be honest, I'm not as big a fan of heroin as the vicar now thinks I am. In fact, I just had to check whether or not heroin was a drug that can actually be injected. I'm still pretty bad-ass though.

Mother was referring to my tattoo addiction rather than anything illegal; I am now well into double-figures. That means I'm very used to dealing with needles touching, scraping and penetrating multiple layers of my skin. I quite enjoy watching tattoos being done too, though I'm not sure how brave I am when it comes to needles going deeper. Or worse; through.

The pain associated with needles is a popular runner for the cause of this phobia, but that's something that doesn't really bother me. I wouldn't go as far as to say that I enjoy the pain, but it's more the purpose of the needle that freaks me out. They are usually either forcing liquids in or out of the body, which is both unnatural and disturbing. I've had a lot of blood tests over the years (because every doctor I visit takes one look at my pigmentless face and thinks I'm anaemic), but I never seem to get used to them. It doesn't help that they put that tight band around your arm to squeeze all the blood to that area; feeling my pulse kind of makes me heave. Then, when they start to take blood away, my body is like "Hey what's the deal with taking something that I'm busy using?" and revolts. Like stealing petrol from a car or some racism from Prince Philip. My hatred of blood tests is probably more to do with fear of blood-removal than of needles.

Our skin is there to protect us; nature's barrier (some more decorated than others, Mother) and so it's not overly accepting of puncture wounds. Any holes in the skin could let the good stuff out, and even a scratch on the skin's surface could lead to infection (and ultimately, death). This phobia has been ingrained into us since Paleolithic times, when simple avoidance of sharp objects would lead to greatly increased chances of survival.

Some 80% of people with this phobia today can name somebody else in their family with the same phobia; which could indicate that some fears are genetic, or could just as easily be attributed to parents projecting their fears onto their young and scarring them for life.

A major symptom of all phobias is a rapid heartbeat, however when it comes to fear of needles, this is often followed by a sudden drop in heart rate, which leads to fainting. Fainting happens when the vagus nerve is triggered, which instantly widens blood vessels and lowers blood pressure. This is also thought to be genetic. As a species who rely on consciousness to react to situations, why have we evolved to pass out during this anxious time? Fainting is much less common with other phobias in humans, but far more common in certain species of goats; who pass out at the mere suggestion of a loud noise.

It is thought that fainting became a defence mechanism thousands of years ago; a nonverbal reaction that shows others that we aren't a threat to them. That makes sense; if someone was coming at me with a sharp object that could take my life, falling to the ground would be my best bet at avoiding confrontation.

In most situations involving needles, it's somebody else who wields the fearful device while we sit idly by. Natural instincts tell you that you are about to be attacked/harmed and so the body reacts in the best way it knows how. Don't be embarrassed if you faint, it means you're tapping into your Paleolithic roots and have the reflexes of a bobcat. An unconscious bobcat. Perhaps a goat!

Although many phobias are dangerous, the sudden changes of physical state around needles makes it one of few phobias that can actually kill. With this phobia, the sudden drop in blood pressure may actually result in death. The number of deaths isn't terrifyingly high, totalling at 23 (ever), but it's still a scary thought.

Despite this phobia being somewhat lethal and needles being a pain in the ass (sometimes literally), I still find it hard to fear them when I've been around them so much.

I'll need to make this challenge scarier for myself somehow…

MY CHALLENGE:

After much contemplation and remarkably little planning, I decided to do something that would be the most painful thing I'd ever put myself through. It also required getting pretty naked in front of a stranger, which definitely adds to the anxiety of the process. Surely there is no better hallmark of the British condition than deeply-ingrained shame of one's disastrously proportioned naked body.

The last time I got something pierced (my earlobes) was when I was about 11 years old and I remember the pain as if it were yesterday. It felt like someone set fire to my earlobes and that intense pain lasted a few days (plus anytime I accidentally caught my ear with the hairbrush afterwards).

Earlobes, as a body part, aren't really that sensitive — you can pinch them pretty hard between your fingertips without feeling uncomfortable (you're totally doing it right now). Imagine the same kind of pain on one of the most sensitive parts of your body; about the same distance apart as your earlobes, but about a foot lower.

Yep. My nipples.

Plus needles.

I feel a bit sick.

Picture a grey, unseasonably cold Monday in June. I was working from my home office when the clock struck 2pm. My list of copywriting tasks for Monday had been completed and all of the housework was done to a very reasonable standard (Mother still wouldn't be allowed in, but to most regular humans it looked fine).

"What an unusual Monday this is, Bandit" I said to the dog, as he licked the place his balls used to be, with sad-eyes. Surely I had missed something? Then I saw it; the pile of ironing that was waiting for me in the washing basket. The stars had aligned and I actually had the chance, nay; the opportunity to do that pile of ironing. Every minute of that morning's productivity had led up to this moment, the moment I could finally wear those linen trousers once more.

I walked excitedly towards the basket and then, out of nowhere, made a swift 90 degree exit out the front door.

I called the piercing place that I'd had saved in my phone book for the entire year; I was drunk on a mixture of ironing-rebellion and unplanned freedom, and I asked her if she had space that afternoon for some nipple stabbing.

She did.

Even her voice terrified me, but we reached a verbal understanding that I was over 16 (my voice gets squeaky when I'm being spontaneous) and I started to power walk towards the studio. This place was the highest reviewed piercing studio in the area; I had done my research. I'm rather fond of having nipples, you see, and I'd hate for them to fall off afterwards.

I called my sister "Hey, fancy a coffee?" She was in. I said "I need to take a small detour first, how strong are you feeling?" she replied "reasonably" which was good news if I needed carrying back home.

When we arrived at the studio, my sister waited outside with the owner while she finished her cigarette. I sat inside, discretely sweating into one of her leather waiting-room chairs.

"Follow me" she said, as I tried to remember how to walk.

I tried not to look at the equipment she was putting together on the tray next to me. I'm very used to tattoo needles, but you can hardly see them when they're fastened to the hefty tattoo machine. These needles were fully exposed (as my breasts soon would be) and I was feeling a bit dizzy. "Let's have a look at you then" she said as she gestured politely to the parts of my jumper that sat closest to her.

I've never been overly shy when it comes to revealing my boobs; I don't think twice about changing in the open spaces of a public changing room. When people say "erm, I can see your nipples in that dress" my response is usually "prize if you spot the secret third one/symmetry is over-rated/are they supposed to be a secret?" However, in front of this very confident, rubber-glove-wearing, roller-derby champion of a lady (I'm not being presumptuous, that's how her nipple piercings were ripped out for the 4th time), I found myself succumbing to uncharacteristic shyness.

The giant wall of witness-your-mutilation-live mirrors placed opposite certainly didn't help.

I hadn't done any research into the process, so I just took it all in my stride and didn't look once. This is what I believe happened: She drew dots either side of my nipples with a pen and then lined up a hand-clamp, which held my first nipple tightly. She then sprayed something absolutely freezing over the area, explaining to me that I would feel it getting colder and colder. Suddenly a sharp pain happened. It was much more bearable than I imagined. Before I could remember to breathe, she fastened the balls onto each end of the jewellery bar (I couldn't feel much at this point) and she covered it in a large plaster. She moved over to the other nipple and kept talking to me the entire time. I loved her a little bit. This may have been early-onset Stockholm Syndrome.

The same process happened again until all I could see were two small white plaster-bandages where my nipples used to be, slowly developing red blobs as blood seeped through the material.

The unusual feeling of numbness made me quite reluctant to return to the warm embrace of my bra, which she highly recommended I did in order to protect them. Once dressed, I hardly noticed the difference.

I was very glad to see my sister smiling at me back in the waiting room. My legs felt a bit shaky, but it was over much quicker than I imagined. Finally the piercer said "enjoy" and gave me a little wink as I left the building. Cheeky.

I bought my sister a coffee, as I initially promised her, but the combination of the warm environment and the warm drink started to 'unfreeze' things. Suddenly a throbbing pain was becoming apparent and I had to fight the urge to cradle myself in the middle of Costa.

I popped some painkillers and headed home pretty fast, praying that I didn't run into anybody who wanted a hug on the way. That happens more often than you'd think in a small city like Lincoln.

Although the whole process (including the pain that followed) was very uncomfortable, especially sleeping, showering and getting undressed, the pride that I felt was worth it. Perhaps it was due to the memento of the occasion. These little metal bars are my trophies.

If anybody else is thinking about getting this done, by the way, I have some words of wisdom for you:

1. Sleep in a bra - seriously, you will wake yourself up when you roll onto one of the piercings. Padded bras are your best friend.

2. The pain lasted 5 full days - professionals say they can take up to a year to heal, which is good to know but when does the throbbing pain stop? For me, day 5 came and I hardly noticed them anymore.

3. Buy an egg cup if you don't have one - this makes two daily salt baths a lot easier. Bending over a normal cup is boring and you end up spilling it all over the floor. I'm super graceful.

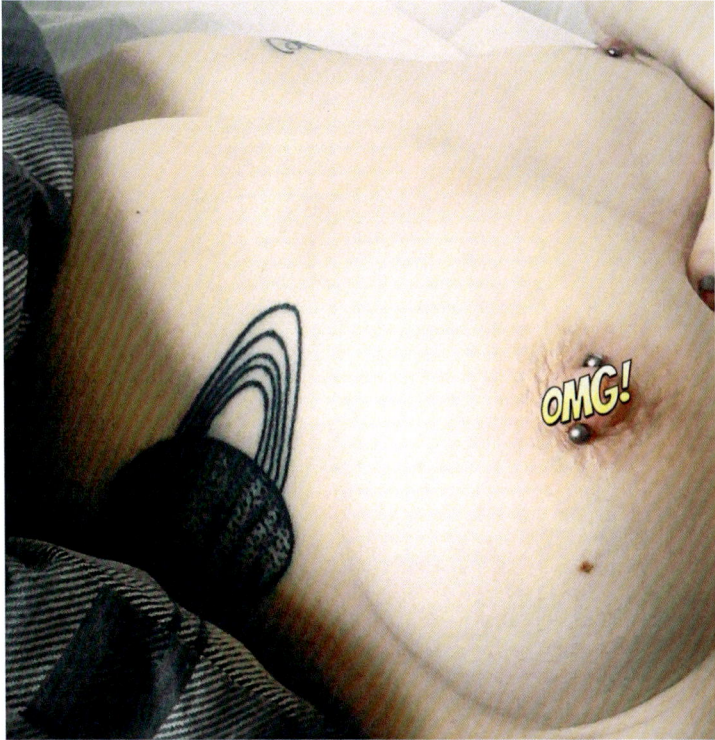

Other things I did that qualify conquering needles:

I suffer from pins and needles every time I cross my legs too hard. I also got 3 more tattoos this year (sorry not sorry).

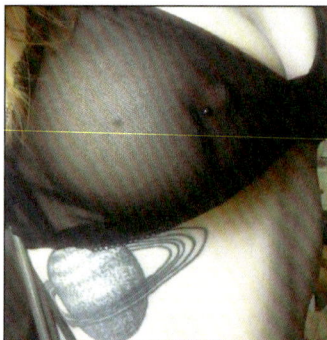

Chapter Five:

Fear 6 – Musophobia

(fear of mice)

Musophobia:

What it is: **Mice**
How rational I think it is: **1/5**
How much I fear it: **0/5**
The date I faced it: **3rd April 2015**
How I conquered it: **Happily**

Rational scale:
0 = irrational, 1 = not very, 2 = relatively, 3 = reasonably, 4 = rational, 5 = very rational

Fear scale:
0 = happy, 1 = easy, 2 = ambivalent, 3 = dislike, 4 = hate, 5 = need new pants

The Phobia:

There are two very different types of mice in the world. There are pet mice that you find curled-up in cute little balls at the pet shop and then you'll find the feral mice; lop-sided creatures that you see ferreting in an old pasty, inside a bin. Rick says that if I was a mouse, I would be the cute one for 25 days of every month.

I can't help but picture an epic 'good vs. evil' battle between Maisy Mouse and the entire crew of Biker Mice from Mars here (the ones with missing eyes and teeth, but absolutely rockin' tiny leather jackets).

Regardless of behaviour (or attire), I think mice are adorable over most other traits. Do the maths; 'fluffy' = cute and 'small' = also cute. So when you combine those two features together, it makes perfect sense that the result is going to be double-cute. Plus, watching a mouse clean behind its ears with those tiny arms is life-changingly beautiful. A simple hygienic gesture like that shouldn't prompt this kind of effect on my ovaries (the same thing happens when I imagine a T-Rex trying to spoon-feed itself some cereal). I just don't see how mice can inflict such fear upon people.

I do understand that feral mice can be quite repulsive. You know, the kind of mice that molt all over the place, are inexplicably greasy or often missing a leg (later found dangling from another one's mouth). Then there's the worst type; the 'intruder mice' that you hear scratching under your floorboards at night and in your food cupboards, staring back at you from the huge hole they've just made in your Sugar Puff box. Like drunk friends at a house party; they've defecated in your Doritos and that's just not cool. I think I'd rather be their next meal than share one with them.

And yet, I'm still not trembling in fear when I see one. So what has caused this common, unusual phobia to emerge?

Mice have been around as long as humans, and can be found in every corner of the globe, which means they are widely-recognised and appear in the media throughout the world. They are renowned for eating and contaminating human food which has given them a bad reputation, understandably, but they are also extremely intelligent. They are natural learners who have the ability to understand and remember different concepts. If you put mice in a maze and lure them to the end with food, they will quickly learn the fastest route and find their way to the treat. This also means they'll remember sneaky entrances into your house and find food storage with scary efficiency.

Mice also excel at climbing, burrowing and chewing anything, anywhere. They're both sneaky and destructive; politicians of the animal world. If they're loose in your house they'll often chew wood and furniture, which is where the famous 'mouse hole in the skirting board' image comes from, and don't get me started on cable chewing. Destroy my ability to watch television and we'll have to have serious words. Stabby, stabby words. Imagine my two cats sitting either side of me like bouncers, too.

Mice tend to only come out at night and hide in dark places, like robbers, rapists, and drug addicts (coincidence?). This all makes it a little clearer as to why it would be a nightmare to find one in your house.

More than 95% of lab tests are performed on rats or mice. They are used in labs for numerous reasons, including the fact that they breed quickly, have short lifespans, are easy to handle and are almost genetically identical to each other. But they are also genetically similar to humans and suffer many similar diseases, enabling scientists to attempt to find cures. Mice also have the ability to crave things and are currently used in trials to research the effects of drug addiction. I assume that the mice start pole dancing for cheese. Ahhh, science.

As much as we associate mice (and rats) with carrying diseases, most famously the Great Plague, successful clinical trials in the pharmaceutical industry mean that at this point they have likely saved far more human lives than we can possibly imagine. Maybe think about that next time you're throwing out a bag of Doritos.

Throw them at me, Chapter Five!

MY CHALLENGE:

Finding mice is a lot harder than you'd think. I could track down a snake in seconds, but mice are a whole different story.

All the biggest pet shops seemed to favour hamsters and rats. I don't get it. Rats, in my mind, are less pet-like than mice. Kids' cartoons are totally to blame for this; where rats are always evil-looking with glowing eyes and living in sewers with a bunch of pizza-eating turtles. In reality, mice aren't sold often because they don't live very long and happen to be secret escape-artists.

I did eventually manage to locate some at a local pet shop. I attempted a casual entrance; asking the staff if they'd mind dousing me with mice. Turns out, that made me look absolutely mental. So I decided to email subsequent shops in advance, minimising the undesirable combination of wanting to hold something that I didn't intend on buying, and facing a popular fear in the process.

I decided to search further afield where I discovered that 'fancy mice' are actually quite a cool thing to collect. There were a few breeders around the country that specialised in both mouseries and fanciness. I emailed a couple of them, but one had recently closed down and the other politely declined my offer to visit them for a quick photograph. Probably for the best; I've been to that part of South Yorkshire before, iPhones with working cameras are considered a muggable offence. It's possible I'm still bitter about it.

Finding mice was turning out to be the hardest part of this plan; something I hadn't even considered. I started to worry about overcoming other phobias too, some of these items would take more hunting down than others. Why are people so afraid of things that are so hard to come by? You would think that would make them less scary.

Just as I was about to travel 3 hours to buy a pair of fancy mice, my mother pointed out (as she so often does) that I was being a moron. There was a farm, less than an hour away from me, that she used to take me to as a child. This farm offered a 'mouse-handling experience' to the general public, daily. I kid you not. It's even labelled like that on their website. Mother had potentially just saved two innocent mice from a year's worth of torture from a hyperactive Jack Russell and two exceptionally wily cats with homicidal tendencies.

So off we went to White Post Farm (Rick and me). Mother declined our invitation to come along, despite offering to buy her some Wotsits for the journey. I was just happy to find somewhere with actual mice.

This was early April-time and lambs were popping out all over the farm. I say 'popping'; it didn't seem quite that simple. The further we explored, the more excited I got about holding the animals. This place was amazing. You could hold chicks, guinea pigs, mice and lambs, and if these animals were even half as excited as the goats that we fed on the way in, we were in for an absolute treat.

If you ever get the chance to; give a lamb a cuddle. I've done that before with lamb chops, on a particularly hungry day, but the real thing is even more satisfying.

The 'meet the animals' section was the last area of the farm tour and consisted of two really long benches. We sat and waited for our chosen animals to be delivered to us from their pen, as patiently as two adults could, and I couldn't help but wonder how some people can't even be in the same room as these tiny animals. Seriously. Children were paying to hold them here.

As the kind lady placed a mouse in my hands, I had to check it had actually landed. I could hardly feel it. In fact, I noticed a wet droplet of excitement that fell out of it a lot more than I noticed the little creature from whence it came. The presence of a squishy brown turd perhaps increased my discomfort levels slightly, but not so much my fear. The mouse was definitely more scared than I was. Poor thing, having to sit next to Rick like that.

I then asked to hold the one that Rick was holding, too; I figured 'a mouse per hand' was a pretty solid way to complete this challenge. If I could have managed a back-flip at the same time, it would have fully illustrated how much I enjoyed this one.

If the puppy hadn't learned to use door handles, I'd definitely buy some as pets, but I find that it's best not to torture things that can carry plagues...

Other things I did that qualify conquering mice:

There was definitely a mouse in the apartment where we stayed in Edinburgh (Rick saw it and I was a bit jealous)... (of the mouse, for living in such a cool place). Also, living with a Jack Russell is kind of like living with a very large mouse – he's fluffy and white, spooks easily and will do anything for cheese.

(The plaster in the photo was not mouse-related.)

Chapter Six:

Fear 5 - Claustrophobia

(fear of small spaces)

Claustrophobia:

What it is: **Small spaces**
How rational I think it is: **5/5**
How much I fear it: **4/5**
The date I faced it: **23rd February 2015**
How I conquered it: **Happily**

Rational scale:
0 = irrational, 1 = not very, 2 = relatively, 3 = reasonably, 4 = rational, 5 = very rational

Fear scale:
0 = happy, 1 = easy, 2 = ambivalent, 3 = dislike, 4 = hate, 5 = need new pants

The Phobia:

Claustrophobia is described as 'the fear of small, enclosed, narrow or confined spaces' which actually surprised me slightly. I generally use this word to describe many more situations, most of which I've purposefully invented at some point. This includes whenever I'm hugged by a tank-top-wearing great uncle with shoulder hair; "sorry… *waves them away* I'm immensely claustrophobic..." then everyone nods and backs away forgivingly. Handy, right? Feel free to use that at family events.

I feel claustrophobic whenever I'm blocked from an escape route or starved of oxygen in some way. This happens surprisingly often; in a queue, on a train, or even when in an open space so vast that I'm suddenly overwhelmed by solitude. Isn't that the most confusing thing? I'm just as uncomfortable when alone as I am when in crowds. The trees that I talk to tell me that I'm probably fine. I'm the same when surrounded by people, especially when it's people I don't know. I've worked out (through frequent uncomfortable dinner invitations) that company of around 2 to 4 people is roughly where my comfort zone is. Unless any of those people are intimidatingly good looking, overly polite, good at maths or any combination of the above.

Rachel Riley (gorgeous Countdown math-genius) doesn't get an invite. She's super obsessed with me.

In terms of rationality, it seems sensible to assume that being trapped in a small space will eventually kill you. Eventually. I imagine that starvation of either fluids or oxygen would do the job, if not the embarrassment of having to soil yourself in a small space. This could be a real issue for me, especially once I start to panic in there. I'll stay in any given scenario long enough to hate it, but not long enough to start hating myself. The same goes for when I'm working my way through the list of starters at Nandos.

Studies have shown that there is often a past event which has allowed this fear to develop. Quite often this is from things like being locked in a cupboard as a child, or getting lost in a supermarket (I, myself, am easily distracted by cookies). Sometimes I get a genuine anxious feeling from just looking at large crowds or windowless rooms on the television, but I've always disliked the feeling of not being able to get out of somewhere; from as early as primary school.

I was briefly hospitalised a couple of years ago (for something mysterious and sexy) (no, not an STD) and none of the nurses could understand why they couldn't get an accurate reading of my pulse. The ward was surprisingly large and relatively empty, but I still felt claustrophobic because I wasn't 'allowed' to leave. My panic attack was confusing medical professionals here, that's how illogical this phobia is!

In the UK, claustrophobia rates are estimated to be double that of American counterparts. Women are twice as likely to suffer from the phobia than men are, too. So, as a British woman, I'm a walking (cowering) target for this stuff. Like many phobias, most people are unaware they have claustrophobia until they are put into a small-spaced situation; a lot of patients have an unexpected panic attack while inside an MRI machine, for example.

The longest tunnel in the world is the Lærdal Tunnel in Norway and is 15.23 miles long. They actually built it with claustrophobics in mind and added three brightly-lit chambers along the tunnel, providing areas for vehicles to turn around in, as well as some open spaces that help lift the feelings of anxiety. Being a relatively debilitating disorder, it's nice to know that people in Norway are taking the matter as seriously as it should be.

I often claim that I was given this phobia by my mother, who for some reason refused to be in small enclosed spaces with me for too long, but studies have shown that claustrophobia doesn't appear to be genetic. The anxious feeling of claustrophobia, however, can be picked up by 50% of children who are exposed to it at a young age. So I can still blame my mother for this. Hoorayyyyy.

Some people have reported their claustrophobia being brought on when they have worn a jumper too tightly (which I immediately committed to memory for the next time I'm arrested for public nudity). "No Officer, I'm just claustrophobic." The excuses just keep on coming.

I am dreading this. I have a feeling that this is going to be a very long challenge, even if it's the shortest. This may be the chapter that kills me, or at least my dignity.

My challenge:

I tried hard to think of the worst small space that I could think of. I figured "if you're going to be uncomfortable, do it properly." Two spaces came to mind. My first thought was an elevator, which is an exceptionally common fear amongst claustrophobics. The second would be one of the most terrifying small spaces to ever wake up in; a coffin.

The coffin was a pretty solid idea because how many nightmares have you had about that situation? There's a myth that in 15th century England they started to run out of spaces in graves. To make some room, they would dig up old bodies and bring them to a bone house. Sounds like a creepy job already, but it gets worse. More often than they would like, the inner lid of these 'used' coffins would be covered in scratch marks. Eurgh. What a horrible way to go. This led to a trend where people wanted to be buried with a string tied around their index finger, attached to a bell above ground (where the term 'dead ringer' comes from). 'The graveyard shift' referred to the person who stayed up all night to listen for noises, and 'saved by the bell' meant, well, you get the idea. So that's a nightmare I have most nights.

I looked into ordering a cardboard coffin online (because

that's how I roll, or won't roll; as the case may be) but, as well as being surprisingly expensive, it felt seriously wrong buying my own coffin. I bet I could chew my way out of cardboard too... I have the jaw of a camel when determined.

Realistically (and moralistically) I didn't want to spend even a second bothering industry professionals with the idea of borrowing a coffin. So I went back to my first thought of an elevator and emailed a couple of building-owners who happened to have one. Despite their very helpful attempts (not sarcasm, for a change) it was understandably against health and safety regulations to spend so much time in one of their oxygen-starved metal boxes. I had to rack my brain for the next best thing; somewhere or something private, where I would be fully to blame if something bad happened to me (panic attacks/pooping; imminent).

Small spaces that people own. Hmm. A loft? A shed? A car? Is there something smaller, preferably dark and with a lock? The car boot?! But of course. Just your run-of-the-mill, kidnapping-scenario.

I texted my brother to tell him him the plan and asked to borrow his car, to which he replied "this sounds easy as Hell", I responded "so's your mum" – and he left me with a timeless and thought-provoking "...", I decided to call her instead. Mum was unexpectedly understanding about this time-wasting idea. "Well, think about it, would you rather be trapped in an elevator or a car boot?" she asked. "I'd take the elevator because then at least you could walk around and stretch your legs." We settled on the boot scenario being the most torturous and so she went outside to clear out her car.

At first glance, this situation didn't seem overly scary. I'd be in a safe place, on a familiar driveway, in a stationary position. However, it would be very cramped, very cold and nobody would be able to hear me if I desperately wanted to get out. It was hard to breathe just thinking about it. (There would be a live-feed GoPro set up in case I actually did have a panic attack).

After much debate about what I was 'allowed' to take into the boot with me, I decided that all I could have was a torch. And my clothing. The torch-light was for the benefit of the GoPro video rather than me. I think I'd actually rather it have been very dark, because then I wouldn't be able to tell how small the space actually was. Plus, in an elevator there would be a light on the whole time anyway, even during a power-cut. Not having my phone on me would be one of the most difficult parts, phone-separation-anxiety is something that scares me almost as much as really being kidnapped.

The car was ready. The GoPro was set up and I had a huge scarf to hide in. All that was left to do was to climb (fall) gracefully (head-first) into the boot. Compared to the two-degree temperature outside, the shelter of the car initially felt quite comfortable. I thought "maybe this wouldn't be so bad." I was all smiles as I waved at my little audience on the driveway.

Then the boot lid was closed. Initial panic set in. It was the kind of panic that comes from knowing that this is only the beginning of something terrible. Similar to when you have food poisoning. I tried to remember that every minute spent in this space was a minute closer to freedom. But, without any kind of distraction, a minute felt like a long, long time.

I reminded myself not to think about my bladder, which only made that desire stronger. I kept telling myself that this was a million times better than being on a plane. I was safely parked on a driveway and alone, rather than thousands of miles in the air surrounded by children and pre-lunchtime-gin drinkers. I could have a hot chocolate in my hand in a couple of hours time.

Positive thinking actually did help. I kept breathing deeply and focusing on hot chocolate, and then the challenge started to get ever-so-slightly easier.

Don't get me wrong; physically I got much less comfortable, but mentally I was improving with every passing moment.

As I shone the torch around my temporary home, I couldn't help but notice some hand prints on the inner lid of the boot. Had Mother actually been kidnapping people? Little bits of dust floated through the rays of torch-light and my knees began to ache; longing to be stretched.

I can't put into words just how much time dragged on. My legs went completely numb, my back ached, the wind shook the car and the rain on the roof kept reminding my bladder that now was an opportune moment to ruin my life.

I memorised the car's manufacturer number, I planned my next five blog posts and I inexplicably had a Blondie song going round and round in my head. Sometimes, between awkward cramps, I almost enjoyed the solitude. I wasn't glued to my phone, I wasn't being jumped on by a teething puppy and I didn't feel obligated to catch up with my client-work. It was at this point that I realised my fear had disappeared and was slowly being replaced with relaxation. I wasn't afraid anymore. I was completely calm.

Eventually I was so calm that I started to feel a bit like I was wasting everyone's time. So when Rick came to check on me after about 2 and a half hours, I decided that spending any more time in my mum's shopping-bag-dungeon would be pointless. Plus, with the immune system of a new-born baby, Pneumonia was becoming a very real threat.

I ached like crazy, but I had learned how to relax my mind. Challenge defeated.

Other things I did that qualify conquering small spaces:

Every single night I am forced to sleep in a space of less-than-a-fifth of the bed. I also didn't enjoy the mirror maze in Camera Obscura; I genuinely panicked when I lost my way out (while forced to look at my own terrified face at every angle).

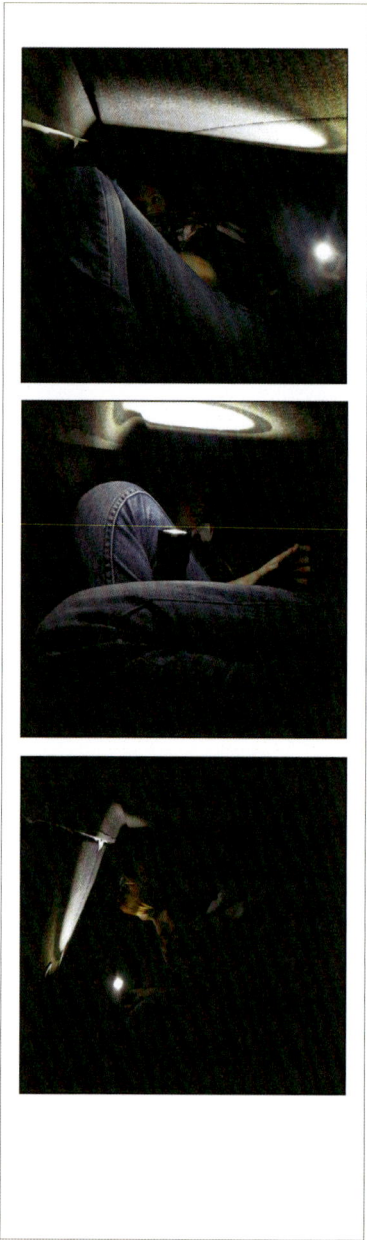

Chapter Seven:

Fear 4 – Arachnophobia

(fear of spiders)

Arachnophobia:

What it is: **Spiders**
How rational I think it is: **1/5**
How much I fear it: **5/5**
The date I faced it: **27th July 2015**
How I conquered it: **Begrudgingly**

Rational scale:
0 = irrational, 1 = not very, 2 = relatively, 3 = reasonably, 4 = rational, 5 = very rational

Fear scale:
0 = happy, 1 = easy, 2 = ambivalent, 3 = dislike, 4 = hate, 5 = need new pants

THE PHOBIA:

Fearing spiders is so stupid! Why do I loathe them this much? Why would I rather burn down my house than remove one from inside it?!

I'm a bit surprised that snakes beat spiders on the fear scale. Spiders might be a lot more common than snakes, but they're a thousand times more terrifying to find in your bath. If you saw a snake in your bath then you'd probably hope that someone was playing a practical joke on you. And, if that was the case, you might want to re-evaluate your friendships rather than your fears.

Logic goes completely out of the window with this fear; UK spiders are very small creatures. The Goliath Birdeater holds the record for the largest-known species of spider; a monstrosity measuring some 11 inches (leg-span). This name 'Goliath Birdeater' makes me picture a giant eight-legged beast living under a bridge, covered in blood and sat on a nest of dead pigeons. In reality this spider is called a 'birdeater' because of an early 18th-century copper engraving that depicts one eating a hummingbird. They rarely prey on adult birds at all. While the thought of an 11 inch spider makes me shudder and vomit a little bit in my own mouth (unrelated sidenote: add Venezuela to my 'places to never-ever-go' list), you could quite easily out-run/squash it in an emergency. So, why do spiders freak so many people out? They are visually similar to many other creepy crawlies, yet others aren't so intimidating. Butter-flies could land on me all day and I'd be ecstatic about it. So what is it about spiders, specifically?

As it goes, spiders have some pretty cool and unique talents. Thousands of tiny hairs allow them to climb up vertical, practically frictionless walls for a start. What did they do to deserve that superpower when they were being dished out?! They also make spider silk with their bum, which is strangely beautiful as well as practical — you may have no-ticed this when they drop down from ceilings directly onto the sandwich that you're about to eat. Seriously though, their silk has proven useful in creating the next generation of parachutes and bullet-proof vests. Spiders are saving lives with their bums. Maybe I should stop trying to flush them down the toilet.

Spiders also have quite a few lesser-known talents that make them even more disgusting, and somehow more impressive. Did you know that they eat the equivalent of the UK population in flies every year? They eat them in a really gross way too; by emptying their stomach liquids into the fly and turning it into fly-soup, before being able to digest it. Imagine how many flies there would be without spiders eating 64.9 million of them each year. It's pretty impressive.

Despite their helpful nature when it comes to de-flying the country, their lack of manners majorly lets them down. It's the way they just casually appear, uninvited, when you're at your most vulnerable (usually on the toilet, putting on your shoes or carrying something heavy). No invitation. No manners. By the time you've gone to grab an empty glass and sprinted back... they've vanished.

A round of applause for the people who can catch and release them back into the wild, unscathed. I either trap one of their legs under the glass and squish it as I drag, or I don't see the spider until it's too late and it becomes a mess under-foot. Sometimes, very occasionally, my aim is perfect and the book I've just thrown hits it square-on. My reflexes might just save me, yet.

In my defence, spiders are both light-footed and leg-heavy, which is a somewhat evil combination that allows them to move extremely quietly and too fast for their own good. As Eddie Izzard once said: "What's worse than seeing a spider? Not seeing a spider!" and I couldn't agree more. I spent a lot of nights afraid to enter my own bedroom because a spider got there first.

Have you ever watched a spider go down the drain in your sink or bath, and breathed a sigh of relief? Me too. Every time. Frustratingly, they are covered in water-repellent hairs that trap a layer of air around the body, keeping them dry and helping them to float. Some can even survive underwater for hours which is why they often crawl back up the drain. One spindly-leg at a time. Ready to avenge themselves.

OK, spiders are impressive/praise-worthy sometimes, I'll admit it. However, I am adamant that they have a vindictive streak, one that gives me decidedly mixed feelings about releasing them back into the wild, versus straight-up killing them. I'm not just talking about their evil intentions towards human beings either (specifically towards me, I'm sure of it), but they are unnecessarily violent towards each other too. Do you know how they breed? Spider reproduction (for the those who don't feel inclined to read up on such things) begins when the male spider stabs his two sperm-laden 'pedipalp' prongs into the female's abdomen. Like some kind of love-grapple-tasering. Male orb-web spiders actually break off the tips of their own genitals and leave their pride and joy inside the female; just to spite any other males who might come along later. Female spiders get their own back though; some species eat the male once they're done with them. "I'm eating for 200 now, get over yourself."

In-between learning about these traits of post-coital cannibalism, turning live prey into soup and their ability to survive some extreme cases of drowning, I've been trying to work out where this particular fear started for me. Surely I wasn't afraid of them as a young child? It's a fear that is extreme and yet doesn't make any logical sense. I can probably pin it down to one particular recurring memory that haunts me every time I see a spider: I always used to sleep with a mug of juice next to my bed and would sip it throughout the night. One morning, as I was clearing the side-table after a particularly thirsty night, I noticed a huge spider sat right at the bottom of the mug. I remember the instant paralysing, mug-dropping dread and instant nausea that followed this observation. There is still a Ribena stain on the carpet to prove it. To this day I pray that it crawled in there after my last sip.

It's fair to say that I'm in no rush to complete this challenge.

My challenge:

The challenge is simple; 'handle' a spider. The same way I imagine I'd handle prison; rocking back and forth in a corner, crying and trying to bribe my way out.

I have a friend who works in a reptile shop but, while the shop owned many Tarantulas, their insurance didn't cover "that kind of thing" and they even advise spider owners not to handle them once purchased. My sure-fire plan had backfired. I had been so confident, so laid back, so at ease. So wrong. I contacted a couple more local reptile shops, but was met with either "out of stock at the moment" or "sorry it's against our health and safety" responses. I sent evidence of this project and mentioned donating money to charity (emphasising the steadiness of my hands, and a willingness to accept non-consensual love-tasering as a valid reproductive method) but nothing seemed to help my case.

I started to look further afield, contacting wildlife centres where children were pictured actually holding Tarantulas on the website. I received the following response: "Although we do have Tarantula's and they do come out into reptile handling sessions we do not let the public hold them. This is because of their delicate nature and we do not want to damage them. Sorry for that." (I left the original poor grammar in that quote because I'm bitter like that). I was genuinely panicking. I tried contacting members of Facebook groups titled 'Tarantula Owners', but no reply. I tried tweeting for help, but no helpful responses. I asked every tattoo artist I knew; many owned snakes but nobody seemed to own spiders. I was feeling very helpless. This was turning out to be harder than finding mice. Twice the number of legs; ten times the work? Even my mum couldn't help with this one.

It was looking like my only option would be to travel 4 hours down to the South Coast and pay £75 to 'Tickle a Tarantula' as part of a Virgin Experience Day. Please never make me say that sentence out loud. Was it do-able? Yes, but not really something I was enthusiastic about, especially since I'd dread the entire prolonged experience.

I left it hanging for a while, hoping that maybe I'd find a huge spider in the garden, one big enough to be impressive. Then, one evening on Facebook, I felt drawn to a name in the sidebar of my 'online friends' menu. This was a guy that I knew had loads of local connections; he does a lot to help local people and businesses, and spends a lot of time in coffee shops/tattoo studios. Those places are full of cool (and slightly unusual) people. People who might own some bizarre pets. I sent Spider-Man (as much as I wish that was his real name, he wishes to remain anonymous) a message:

"I don't suppose you know anyone with a Tarantula, do you?"

His response gave me instant, immeasurable hope:

"Yeah. What species of Tarantula do you have in mind – something to hold or big fangs? Any colour preferences?"

That first word would have been enough, but I was being given the foreign concept of Tarantula-choice. Beautiful, beautiful, choice! Not only was this guy going to collect the spider for me, he was going to choose the most friendly one and bring it to my local coffee shop, in the rain. The rain wasn't planned, but it made the gesture even more valiant.

After all of this stress, I was mostly just glad to have a Tarantula available to me, so I hadn't given much thought to the actual holding-process. Unbelievably, before I knew it, there was a two-year-old Chilean Rose Tarantula sat staring at me through a foggy-plastic container. Her huge, hairy legs made my skinny, hairy legs go weak and my skin crawled to the rhythm of her steps. It was a horrible feeling. She seemed very content in her box and I wasn't in any rush to encourage her out of it.

I decided to stall the process by asking Spider-Man some questions.

The spider had a slight pink tinge to her torso (the Rose part of her name, so I'm told) and she was actually quite pretty. When asking what her name was, Spider-Man chuckled to himself and said "she's called Fanny — because she's pink and hairy." Poor Fanny; she had neither the self-awareness nor ears to appreciate the brilliance of her own name.

I was given a few warnings about Fanny's defence moves. If she raised her front legs it meant she felt threatened and was likely to bite me, like when you try to take a pint glass off a drunk lady in Wetherspoons. I was also told to avoid touching the back of her abdomen, to avoid sharp hairs being shot out with an intention to blind predators. This was around the time that I decided to put my glasses on. Finally, I knelt beside the table and waited patiently and still(-ish) for her to leave the comforts of her container.

She moved quicker than I expected; feeling for her surroundings and climbing onto Spider-Man's hand, who offered her towards me instantly. Great. My hand was clammy but surprisingly solid as I joined the hand-queue. She paused for a while before taking a long, light step onto my palm. One small step for Fanny and one giant leap for Spadge. Yes, I just compared the significance of this moment to the moon-landing. No, I won't apologise.

It was hard to contain the shiver that crept up my spine at that moment; every bone in my body told me to move my hand away, but at this point I was painfully eager to get this over with.

Fanny was totally in control of the situation. We moved with her rather than encouraging her in a certain direction. She started to walk up our arms (half on me and half on Spider-Man) and we found ourselves completely at her mercy. "Not towards our faces, Fanny, I'm begging you." She seemed to listen and started to walk back towards my open palm. She knew exactly where she wanted to go and continued to walk left, I now had sole custody of her and had to quickly move my hands to keep up with her. She looked much bigger outside of her container.

I was so distracted by the prospect of keeping her safe that I completely forgot about my own fear. She sat happily between both of my palms for about 15 minutes and I was reluctant to disturb or aggravate her. She was so comfortable, in fact, that when we eventually had to try and tip her back into her container, she didn't want to go.

Hovering over the box was tricky because my hands were an awkward way round and, as I tilted her gently backwards, I felt evidence of those super-grippy spider feet for the first time. Human skin was no match for her spider-grip. It was such a weird feeling – it almost stung, like sharp Velcro being dragged over you against the grain. I couldn't get her off fast enough, but I remained calm and was very happy that the experience was coming to an end.

She was a beautiful creature and I'm very grateful to have met her. It seems this experience is much rarer than I initially thought, so I tried to appreciate it as much as I could. It's nice to know you're one of few to experience something like this and it was an even better feeling to have overcome this fear. I could do this again now, for sure. Just as long as I never have to touch a rogue one inside my house.

Thank you, Fanny, for not blinding me or giving me another piercing. And I can't thank Spider-Man enough, I hope he reads this. He completely came to my rescue, going so far out of his way to help. It restored my faith in the kindness of people who owe you absolutely nothing in life.

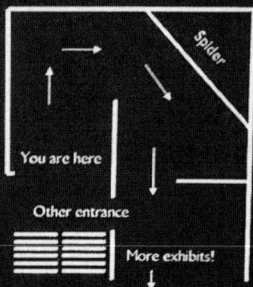

- CAUTION -
SPIDER!

Arachnophobes beware -
there is a giant spider just
around the corner

Parents are advised that
there may be some scary
pictures in the hologram
gallery - to skip this
section take the main
door to your right

You are here

Other entrance

Spider

More exhibits!

Other things I did that qualify conquering spiders:

Nope.

Actually, while visiting Camera Obscura in Edinburgh (May) - I came across this sign (see opposite).

This fear of spiders is so real that Camera Obscura decided to warn people about a 3D image of one. Amazing. I totally looked that image straight in the eye.

Chapter Eight:

Fear 3 - Glossophobia

(fear of public speaking)

Glossophobia:

What it is: **Public speaking**
How rational I think it is: **3/5**
How much I fear it: **5/5**
The date I faced it: **24th May 2015**
How I conquered it: **Nervously**

Rational scale:
0 = irrational, 1 = not very, 2 = relatively, 3 = reasonably, 4 = rational, 5 = very rational

Fear scale:
0 = happy, 1 = easy, 2 = ambivalent, 3 = dislike, 4 = hate, 5 = need new pants

The Phobia:

Some people are great at public speaking. You can separate these superhumans from the mortals by the fact that they're not standing in a puddle of sweat by their second sentence.

I hate these people. I hate anybody who is brave under public pressure. Yet, I've seen some great examples: best man speeches, live comedians, enthusiastic conference speakers who can't seem to draw Venn diagrams fast enough... Seriously. Stop it. These guys have been born in the wrong millennium; they should be leading tribes into battle.

There was this one guy at a franchising event I went to a couple of years ago that I'll never forget. He got so excited about public speaking that he actually interrupted another public speaker by climbing on stage. He was like "Sorry, can I just say something here..." he Kayne'd the crap out of this presentation and nobody was complaining. He was awesome. He started drawing on this flip chart like he was playing the last board of Pictionary, throwing impressive facts at us like rock stars throwing drumsticks out to the crowd. He was in his element, he owned the floor so much that by the end of his speech I had forgotten how to applaud. How does someone find the bravery to do something like that?

In order to survive in prehistoric times, we were dependant on our ability to be accepted into a strong group (for our own protection). So if someone made the terrible decision to stand on a rock in front of everyone, they would create the ideal opportunity to say something stupid. This would be followed by banishment from the group and succumbing to a very lonely death. That is why our brains tell us to fear public speaking – humiliation and a slight case of premature death. The larger the audience, the more people who can reject you.

Tribe chiefs, teachers and world leaders are excused from this kind of speech-ban; they are confident in their messages and rarely indulge in Jägerbombs. But I think public speaking for 'followers' should be banned. Just take a look at YouTube threads on the Internet; those people should not be allowed to talk to other human beings. Ever.

I'm haunted by memories of a girl that once passed wind uncontrollably and another that once fainted and landed on the headteacher's crotch. An audience can conjure up cruel nicknames pretty damn fast ('head-girl', ha ha. OK; that was pretty good). Who would want to subject themselves to such public ridicule like that? If I had the choice to sit on a plane for 60 minutes or speak in front of a large audience for 60 seconds, I would find it extremely hard to pick one (then I'd purposefully try to get into an accident just large enough to render both tasks impossible).

In many American surveys, public speaking comes at the very top of the list of fears:

"According to most studies, people's number one fear is

public speaking. Number two is death. Death is number two. Does that sound right? This means to the average person, if you go to a funeral, you're better off in the casket than doing the eulogy." – Jerry Seinfeld

Ahhh comfy, comfy caskets. Sometimes, speaking is the most effective way of getting your message across, though. If you need to tell somebody to move their car because it's blocking you in, for example, then a fax isn't going to get you home by midnight. When public speaking is your best (or in this case: only) option, it might help to take some advice from one of the greatest speakers in history:

Martin Luther King truly captivated his audience in one of the most famous speeches of all time: "I have a dream…" which he made in 1963. His words have become timeless and what most people don't realise is that King bailed on the speech he had written. A close friend in the audience, Mahalia Jackson, shouted to him: "tell 'em about the 'dream'" and the rest is history. King opened up from his heart and spoke to his audience as if they were a close friend; not just making, but changing history.

It pains me that I lack the confidence to shout "help" in a situation where I am close to death. I don't even like talking when I'm totally inebriated or have a brilliant idea to share during a meeting (sometimes those last two happen at the same time). I usually just email everyone while we're all sat around the same table. I also turn a delightful shade of cherry tomato when people stare at me, which makes the whole situation even more uncomfortable. I'm like a beacon of red light that's illuminating my own discomfort.

This challenge is going to be as hard for the audience as it is for me.

My challenge:

One of my best friends got married to the love of her life in May, congratulations Heatherbelle and Beanochops! Yeah, my friends are kind of forced to adopt Care Bear names. It's endearing. Shut up. I'd only just met the groom that day, but this wedding was the biggest event in my calendar this year. Without exception.

I was excited to witness such a historic moment, but I was even more excited when asked to be maid-of-honour/dinner-speech-maker, along with the third leg of our friendship-tripod: Elibear.

This wedding made history in two ways; last-names changed AND minds were blown (by the speech). It was the ideal opportunity to nail this public speaking challenge. And possibly a bridesmaid.

A bridesmaid's speech may be perceived as a little strange and not the most traditional affair at a wedding, but as a three-way friendship, we have always ignored most traditions. Who decided that best friends come in twos, anyway? We complain that shops don't sell triple beds, that elaborate slow-dance routines are built for two and that train seating is set out in pairs. Screw you, monogamous-society and all your torrid affectations...

A wedding-party audience is often one of the most difficult crowds to entertain. It's a combination of partly-drunk teenagers and partly-deaf grandparents; leaving you with a very varied crowd to please in the space of just a few short minutes. Writing the speech was almost as hard as performing it, and we didn't have any time to practice either.

I was lucky to be surrounded by very supportive friends, if anything can get you through torture, I believe that true love can.

With a best friend either side and a strong drink in hand, it was time to perform the speech. I picked up the cue cards (excellent job Elle, for making those cue cards bullet-point-less; you have always been a mega-babe) and waited for the introduction from the Father of the Bride. I was stood behind the head-table, a wall and two girls in high heels; running was no longer an option. Especially after two glasses of champagne. I was barricaded in position.

Elle very kindly agreed to start the speech, which took the pressure off me a lot. As she spoke, I simply focused on breathing and attempted to look past the audience of about 80-100 eyeballs, rather than directly at them. Elle was amazing. She was honest and confident, and she wasn't even holding her cue cards. I tried to mimic her gestures in my mind, in an attempt to match her skill, but then I noticed something.

She had gone off script.

I started to panic. She was doing a Martin Luther King! All of my inner voices shouted "Bail, Spadge, abort!"

I could no longer follow where she was, and I had no idea when I was supposed to come in. I had no choice but to roll with her. And she was rolling fast!

At first it was absolutely terrifying, but slowly it became natural as we settled into a rhythm rather than spluttering over trembling cue cards. I felt so proud of us right then. Even as the speech continued. We weren't just reading, we were telling the truth; sharing our story. We started to help each other; when she paused – I swooped in – and she did the same with me. Beautiful teamwork.

We smiled at each other, we smiled at the bride and groom, and we smiled at the audience. There was a lot of smiling. They laughed along at all the right places and by the time they were applauding, it all seemed to be over so quickly.

In fact, if there wasn't photographic evidence of this happening, then I think I would have blanked it out completely.

I don't know if it was the adrenaline (or the alcohol) but I've never fallen in love with an entire room full of people, all at the same time before. Probably the alcohol. Right then in my mind, the second hardest challenge for me was now over, and all I could think about was how much I wanted to do it again.

Despite saying a lot of stupid things in the speech (very deliberately, I should add for context), I was glad to not be banished from the group, post-speech.

Other things I did that qualify conquering public speaking:

I quite regularly give an embarrassingly large food order to a waiter in front of an entire table of people (sometimes the whole restaurant can hear if I'm very excited about it). I also talked my mum into auditioning for BBC's Bargain Hunt this year, we auditioned, we gave a speech, we conquered. We couldn't make the filming dates.

Chapter Nine:

Fear 2 – Ophidiophobia

(fear of snakes)

Ophidiophobia:

What it is: **Snakes**
How rational I think it is: **4/5**
How much I fear it: **2/5**
The date I faced it: **14th August 2015**
How I conquered it: **Enthusiastically**

Rational scale:
0 = irrational, 1 = not very, 2 = relatively, 3 = reasonably, 4 = rational, 5 = very rational

Fear scale:
0 = happy, 1 = easy, 2 = ambivalent, 3 = dislike, 4 = hate, 5 = need new pants

THE PHOBIA:

I don't particularly dislike snakes (despite them regularly ruining childhood board games involving ladders); I find them quite intriguing. Still, you wouldn't find me rushing to approach one, unless it was behind multiple layers of glass or draped elegantly around a beautiful tattooed man.

It surprises me that snakes appear so highly in this phobia list, not only because they're low on my own list but because you rarely see them in the UK. They are definitely out there though; snakes inhabit every continent of the world except Antarctica. Here in the UK, we actually have some of the safest native species in the world (although, if one escapes from a local zoo, that's a bit more of an issue). This is reassuring compared to a popular travel destination like Australia, which is home to no fewer than 7 of the world's 10 deadliest snakes. You can't escape spiders anywhere in this country, but I have never seen a snake outside of a cage until this year.

So why, as a nation, are we so scared of them?

Is it the scaly texture? Is it the slithery movements? They move surprisingly fast for something without appendages of any kind and they sure are creepy looking. They're basically a long neck with a lot of teeth at one end and the (admittedly rather desirable) ability to dislocate their jaw and eat everything whole. They can digest giant rabbits, baby deer or even a crocodile, whenever they feel like it. I bet they even eat babies in some countries, though I'm reluctant to check.

Weirdly, in Shfaram (Northern Israel) in 2012, a one-year-old bit the head clean off a 13-inch coin snake! Hell yeah. That was totally the opposite kind of story I expected to find while researching 'snake bites baby'. That's an awesome kid right there, thank you for making my research less depressing.

Snakes also have a pretty poor reputation. Have you ever seen a nice snake portrayed in the media? It has been recorded that snake bites kill up to 100,000 people a year and a total of 400,000 are left disabled or disfigured by their injuries. Those numbers are probably even larger, because some of the most deadly snakes are in countries that don't keep data or records of these things.

Luckily, there's only one deadly species that's native to Britain; the Adder, which has the most highly developed venom injecting mechanism of all snakes. A terrifying fact but even then; they're not aggressive by nature, so you just have to watch where you step and maybe don't call their girlfriend fat (unless she's just eaten your baby).

Snakes are always cast in a derogatory role in stories, too. In the Jungle Book – evil hypnotist snake. In Aladdin – Jafar turns into an evil snake. Enough of the Disney references, Spadge. OK, OK, what about The Bible then? Snakes are just very slippery by nature; would Adam and Eve have been banished from Eden if there had been no talking snake? No talking snake? Don't be ridiculous, Spadge. The Bible would be unrealistic without it. Some say it was the devil inside the snake, but I still feel pretty shady about trusssssssting snake-advice now. The combination of t, folk-lore and the majority of media coverage, all point towards snakes being malicious and deadly.

The thing that makes snakes fear-worthy is their teeth and, in some specimens, the venom inside/surrounding the teeth *raises an eyebrow expectantly at your impressed reaction* oh yes, I know my snake-anatomy. I imagine that death would be the worst consequence of encountering a snake, but there's also the likelihood of severe pain or loss of limbs; day-ruiners for sure.

There are two types of snake venom that you'll find in a snake bite; hemotoxic and neurotoxic. The former affects the blood and the latter affects the nervous system. Hemo-toxins destroy red blood cells, preventing the blood from clotting and will shut down organs, whereas neurotoxins paralyse their victims by attacking the nervous system and muscles.

The venom of Adders is largely neurotoxic, but even if you do get bitten by an Adder in the beautiful English countryside, their venom is not strong enough to be fatal. Nobody has died from an Adder bite in over 20 years, the most common side effects are dizziness and vomiting. If you do not attempt to handle or harm it, then you should be safe. It is also an offence to harm or kill them, so it's best to be nice to these creatures.

Just to be safe, regardless of where I see a snake, I feel that there's really no need for me to disrupt it from its very busy day of persuading passing women to try an apple.

Even their own skin can't stand them.

Here goes nothing.

My challenge:

Hold a snake. That's right; not just poke it or stroke it, ahem, but fully embrace it. I'd probably also let one mildly restrict blood flow to my hand if any sudden hero-like tendencies decide to make an appearance.

Snakes, as it turns out, are very easy to get hold of. Not just physically, but because family-based animal parks are very happy to let you hold them. I guess snakes are a bit more friendly than spiders, as well as more robust? They move slower and I imagine it's quite hard to drop a snake (especially when it wraps itself around you). Whatever the reason, any member of staff I spoke to were only too happy to help me with this challenge. If the cages were big enough, I'd have probably been allowed to get in there and spoon one.

So, on a dreary afternoon in March, I turned up at a 'reptile handling' slot at the Woodside Wildlife & Falconry Park in Lincoln, to accept my fate. I was quite surprised that they don't check your animal-handling background, I could have been a serial-squeezer.

I sat next to some snivelly, impatient school children and, with all the self-control I could muster, I waited for my turn. You can't steal these kinds of opportunities from children; the teachers glare at you, the kids start crying and before you know it you're being asked to leave for teaching the children new 'big girl' words. This happens every single day at this wildlife park (the reptile-handling, rather than my imagination running riot with ideas of those children and their proximity to the duck pond). I could touch their boa constrictor every day, if my plans for world-domination could be put on hold. Why had I never done this before?

After what felt like an eternity of fake-smiling at teachers, the snake was passed over to me. It was every bit as awesome as I expected. It was drier to touch than I thought it would be, in fact it looked a bit 'flaky' in places and as it wrapped its muscular body around my arm, I was eager to find out some more about him. My first question "when did he last eat?" followed by "why is he looking at me like that?" were met with chuckles from the staff. Nobody ever takes my science questions seriously. I discovered that boa constrictors are one of the largest snakes in the world (the longest one ever found was 18 feet), but this one was pretty young and only about 3 feet long.

I was quite comfortable wearing him like a full-arm brace-let, in fact it kind of made me sad when he was taken away. It was like being disrupted from a hug before you've quite finished enjoying it. I'd be even happier to hold one again in future now, although it's important to remember what mother says: "just because you found a polite, gym-going snake doesn't mean you should touch strays…"

I left this experience feeling a little bit, underwhelmed?

Was it because I'd actually enjoyed the challenge and had a lovely day out? Possibly. Or was it because a bunch of kids had done the exact same thing seconds before me? Either way, I felt a bit deflated.

Isn't it funny how life works out, though. While completing one of the other challenges in early August, a press photographer got talking to my sister and boyfriend about my project. Before I knew it, I had a local paper wanting to write a feature about what I was doing, and they wanted to take their own photograph for this feature too. This was a great opportunity for some local publicity, but they wanted me to hold either a snake or a spider in this photograph. After explaining the massive amount of trouble I had previously, when trying to hunt down a spider, they agreed that a snake would be perfect (and I was much happier about that), so I tried to come up with a plan.

The Wildlife Park, where I held one in March, was a few miles out of Lincoln. So to make life easier I emailed a local reptile shop – L.A Reptiles, which is run by some awesome, awesome people. They were more than happy to oblige; replying to my message with a simple and cool "Yeah sure, just let us know when." I told them a time and date, and showed up not quite knowing what to expect.

Their shop is fascinating (and a little bit creepy); it's dark, warm and full of all sorts of reptiles, but what really stole my attention was a pet raccoon called Roscoe that sat in the back of the shop. He was happily playing with some kind of shiny metal object and rolling around in what looked like a sand pit.

"Sweet raccoon!"

"Thanks, it's a little shit."

"Awesome."

I can't tell you how nice everyone was, they offered me drinks, they offered to dress up as clowns and, most importantly, they let me hold five snakes for the photograph. Five. At once. Not only that, but these infant snakes hadn't left the shop before and this photograph was being taken outside, in the rain.

All I could say at this point was was "Five? As in, more than one?" – blowing everyone away as usual. That's a lot of teeth. I was suddenly feeling a little bit nervous for the first time. I could deal with one at a time. Large, frequently-held snakes are wonderfully calm, but five young ones? At once? Wriggling everywhere? Send help.

As soon as the photographer arrived, one of the shop guys practically ran over to the glass cage. Everybody was excited. When shop-guy reappeared, his hands were full of what I can only describe as a blur of small snakes. They were going crazy, slithering in all directions and climbing him like a tree. He looked like he'd just given Medusa a hair-cut. These things didn't stay still even for a second. Despite being no girthier than chipolatas, they could currently eat entire mice in one-go. What would they eat in a few more months? Puppies? Sheep?

I waited until we were all in position before holding my hands out, ready to tackle this weird amalgamation of snake-faces. The snake handler had to keep rearranging them in his arms so that they didn't slither straight onto the floor. I was so terrified of dropping them. 'Clumsy' and 'brave' do not sit well together in newspaper headlines. Holding these snakes was not going to be as easy as it was the first time and I don't think children would enjoy this experience as much (yep, still competing). Part of me was very happy that this had become more of a challenge, yet part of me felt suddenly very needy towards this shop guy. "Don't leave me alone with your snake babies!"

Holding onto them was impossible. They wanted to hide somewhere warm out of the rain and slithered in all directions. I almost forgot about the photographer at this point, but she kept shouting at me "hold them closer to your face" and "look horrified." I don't know if you've ever tried to put a frantic baby snake near your face but they really like to flail around near your eyes. At one point I had a snake-head inside my mouth. They slithered up, around my neck and there was a very awkward moment where shop-guy had to remove one from down my cleavage. The photographer was having so much fun "put one in her hair!", "can you make them all look at her at once?" I'm not entirely sure what she expected from this regular human being; the ability to communicate with live animals? But I was too busy focussing to argue.

It's amazing how quickly I got used to them being on me. At first I was quite timid around them, afraid to grip them too tightly and reluctant to put them too close to my face. You had to hold them forcefully. If you didn't then they'd be on the floor in seconds. Getting the best photo became our top priority, and so all other issues became pointless. "Stick one around my neck? Sure." "Give one a kiss? I know this game." Trying to maintain smooth hair in the rain also became ridiculous, so I let my 'Crazy Snake

Lady' appearance come out.

Despite the rush of having to do this on my lunch break, the terrible weather and the somewhat unusual requests of the photographer, I loved every second. I feel like we bonded on a visceral level (possibly because at some point or another, they were inside me).

It's crazy to think that these tiny snakes would grow up to be about 17 feet long some day. I hope all five of them live long and happy lives, and I hope they don't ever eat Roscoe.

Second biggest fear; conquered.

Other things I did that qualify conquering snakes:

I approached (fearlessly, I might add) a very snake-like stick in the park. I also ate a questionably long hot-dog and touched another snake at White Post Farm. Though that last one was just a quick prod.

Chapter Ten:

FEAR 1 - ACROPHOBIA

(fear of heights)

Acrophobia:

What it is: **Heights**
How rational I think it is: **5/5**
How much I fear it: **4/5**
The date I faced it: **8th August 2015**
How I conquered it: **Unsteadily**

Rational scale:
0 = irrational, 1 = not very, 2 = relatively, 3 = reasonably, 4 = rational, 5 = very rational

Fear scale:
0 = happy, 1 = easy, 2 = ambivalent, 3 = dislike, 4 = hate, 5 = need new pants

The Phobia:

Well, Britain's biggest fear. Congratulations heights, you made it to the very top (ha) of the phobia pile. Nicely chosen, Britain. Heights may not be top of my own fear list, but they are definitely in the upper half. I think they are a fine choice.

Being a long way from the ground is a bad place for anyone to find themselves; somehow you have reached a location that is unnaturally safe for a wingless mammal. Only one mammal can fly; the bat, and the only thing that you have in common with the mighty bat is that you're bat-shit crazy if you are enjoying a situation this dangerous. The bat also has somewhat-impaired vision. So I imagine that must be the only excuse they have for their defiance towards the more logical of mammal traits (i.e. never leaving the safety of a solid surface).

No matter how safe you feel, knowing that you're high up always fills you with an element of danger. And that's only natural; it's an instinct that has allowed us to survive as a species. Being somewhere at height could lead to a fall and falling often leads to death, or at the very least some form of mild discomfort. Both terrible consequences that are best avoided. Although closely related, the fear of falling (basophobia) is considered a fear of the sensation rather than the height that precedes it. I can definitely add basophobia to my own personal top 10 phobia list. I'm not keen on motion, in general, actually. I think we'd all be much happier in a country of bungalows and those milk floats that rarely go above 20mph. What's that? I should be Prime Minister? Oh stop it.

Even if you're inside somewhere that is high up but stable and secure – like the top floor of The Shard building – where you feel pretty safe, it's still only false security. There are a lot of bad things that could happen to you before you reach the safety of the exit on the ground floor. What's to stop you falling down the stairs? Don't say "handrail." What if the elevator fails and you're trapped there for hours with impatient tourists? What if a lion escaped from London Zoo and sets up camp in the stairwell? It could be days before you get back outside into the sweet, fresh London air *chokes on smog*. See, this is what my mind does in every situation; it imagines the worst scenarios and then screams them out to me over and over again until I have to lie down in the middle of IKEA.

It happens to the best of us.

You only have to visit YouTube once before you're bombarded with videos that are nothing but montages of people doing crazy stuff on top of buildings, constantly falling off or over things. Just 30 seconds into one of these videos and it's clear to see that heights are a really bad idea (as well as still playing an important role in natural selection).

Humans are ingrained to avoid things that could lead to death or injury, so those that live without any kind of fear of heights are more likely to die out. As survivors, we are the logical, we are the wise. Yet, I'm now more annoyed to be shit-scared of ladders.

Perhaps it's easier to blame gravity. The great Isaac Newton said "what goes up must come down" and this high level (lol, I'll stop.) of realisation was so terrifying that it gave one of the brightest minds in the world a nervous breakdown. Newton was a knight for goodness sake, and the concept of 'falling' broke him. Gravity is confusing to be fair; it takes speeds of 7 miles per second to escape its hold (on Earth), yet drop a tiny magnet next to a fridge and it's like "gravity who?" I've come up with my own theory; that heights would be fine if the ground wasn't the neediest thing on the planet – "The further you are from it, the more likely it is to harm you."

If only the same rule applied to Ryan Gosling... FOR GOODNESS SAKE, RYAN; GET ON THIS TANDEM WITH ME AND TELL ME I'M PRETTY. FOR YOUR OWN SAFETY.

In the battle of Spadge vs. gravity, my money is on the unstoppable force.

My challenge:

It turns out that I'm a lot more scared of heights than I realised. This is mostly due to feeling claustrophobic rather than unsafe, though. Once up high and away from the majority of civilisation, it's not a quick-fix to return to the comfort zone. That's the main problem for me.

I feel like I conquered this challenge once already in May; when visiting the highest point of Lincoln Cathedral. To some extent, that might even be more impressive, but either way, I did this task twice for good measure.

The highest tower of Lincoln Cathedral stands at 470 feet above sea level and 240 feet above ground (that's 44 times my height and about 17 double decker buses). It was a very difficult challenge for me, not just standing at the top; but making it to the top! I'm pretty unfit, it's true, but I'm mostly referring to the incredibly tight-spaced spiral staircase (barely wide enough for one person, even with my slim frame). The stairs just kept coming. It was almost pitch-black in places and the steps themselves were painfully uneven. Reaching the fresh air at the top actually became quite a welcoming experience, despite feeling very dizzy after the twists of the climb.

However, when this accomplishment was met with the decidedly underwhelming response of "so you just climbed up some stairs?", I felt hugely frustrated that it wasn't an impressive enough feat. Lincoln Cathedral was the highest building in the world for about 300 years (and it really does feel it during the climb) but I refused to have my huge, final challenge met with such a disappointed response.

Panicking slightly, I tried hard to find high places that weren't specifically buildings, many of which were in large built-up cities and popular venues that hundreds of people go to, daily. If hundreds of people were doing it, I feel like it's just not that impressive. I needed a challenge that didn't involve sharing my triumph with thousands of other people.

I have been on a tour of the Eiffel Tower, which I remember struggling with, but there were so many railings and other people around that it was actually quite difficult to see anything, anyway. Not that I went anywhere near the edge.

I wanted something more unusual. I considered taking a helicopter or hot air balloon ride, but that merged heavily into the 'flying' category. I needed something more specific to heights. Climbing up somewhere high (without stairs), perhaps something like abseiling. A bungee-jump would mean repeating the terror face-down and was a lot like 'falling'. I don't need that extra nausea in my life, thanks.

As if brought to me by fate, I spotted an article in the local paper. The title read:

"Daredevils handed unique opportunity to abseil down Lincoln Cathedral."

That meant abseiling from the highest point of the Cathedral's indoor ceiling. At the highest point, I'd be hanging 98 feet above ground with nothing between me and the floor. Just plenty of cold, unsupportive air. Plus, I will be one of very few people (45) to complete this once-in-a-lifetime experience. I was determined, but I had to move fast.

After leaping across all hurdles by emailing the organisation directly, I sent an instant booking fee and received a confirmation letter five days later. It was official: at 12.45pm on the 8th of August, I would be abseiling 98 feet inside one of my favourite buildings in the world.

The euphoria of winning a limited place on the abseil list didn't last long. As a little bit of realisation appeared, so did a little bit of poo.

What made this challenge slightly more stressful was the fact that it couldn't be rescheduled for any other day. I had one shot to do this; one time slot, and I had to be in peak physical health (something that rarely happens when I'm anxious). Unusually, I seemed to be in some kind of denial about the whole thing. I even woke up at 3am the morning of the challenge, but then drifted smoothly back to sleep. No Horlicks required.

I was still completely easy-going later that morning, too. I think perhaps my mind was creating some kind of sub-conscious coping-mechanism. Ahh, sweet, comforting, blind-denial. As midday approached, I had a last-minute idea to buy one of those iPhone armbands, you know the ones that people wear while jogging because their running tights don't have pockets? This meant that I could take my phone with me and I could 1) call Rick from the top if I needed a pep-talk (most likely), 2) get a photo of the view from the top and 3) count the minutes until I was back on the ground.

After some awkward salesy-conversation with the 16 year old, orange-coloured gym-child who served me the overpriced armband (apparently it was neon-yellow or neon-green and nope; £25 wasn't a joke price), it was time to head to Lincoln Cathedral.

Meticulously following instructions as always, I arrived at the door 35 minutes early, ready to fill out a handful of forms. Media releases for the press, mostly. That took me all of four minutes and I could tell that the lady in the charity tent was getting annoyed at my many questions. It turns out that we went up to the drop in groups of six. I wasn't sure if I found this more comforting or more terrifying. On the one hand, we were 'in it' together and could support each other at the top, on the other hand, it meant that 5 strangers may soon see me throw-up.

While I waited, the charity lady encouraged me to go and watch some of the group who were currently abseiling. This sounded like a great idea; I could get some tips from the people who had just done it. In hindsight, this was a bloody terrible idea. Some people came down in tears, some screamed at the top, while others came down uncontrollably spinning on the rope. One lady had her shoes confiscated, and at one point a rogue glove was dropped from the top and the crowd below gasped. Honestly, the fear that echoed throughout the crowd still haunts me.

As the first abseiler reached the bottom, they were met with a huge round of applause (from everyone except me that is, I was sporting my 'applying mascara' face; mouth open and eyebrows raised to the ceiling).

At this point, the older gentleman to my right turned and said to his wife "who the hell would do this?" and I couldn't help but exclaim (somewhat embarrassed) "I'm actually in the next group..." He handed me a £5 note from his pocket and said "Good luck, love, please accept this donation." With tears in my eyes and a new-found admiration for strangers (especially grumpy-looking old people). I kissed my family goodbye and, with my new neon-iPhone strap cutting off the circulation to my arm, I power-walked back towards the meeting point.

There was now a group of three waiting by the charity tent: a mother and daughter combo, and an older guy wearing a T-shirt with a picture of a lady on it. We were mostly nervous, pacing back and forth a little, and when the charity girl offered everyone some jelly babies, I was the only one to accept. I then spent a few seconds explaining to the group why the manufacturer covers the jelly babies in cornflour (to stop them sticking together in the packet) after which I discovered that there was, in fact, a whole new level of awkward-silence left to discover. Good work, Spadge; making friends for life with your confectionery geekery. In the bag.

As the final two people turned up, a safety guy came to stop me from murdering all conversation and talked us through using the harnesses. He also made us tie our hair back and wear a helmet that came down below our eyebrows – I was starting to regret signing those media releases.

As the last set of safety gloves were delivered to our group, it was time to climb up the clock tower. This is the tower just below the bells, just under half-way from the highest-point. I stood at the very top of the tower earlier this year, and the climb was a serious mission. I imagined that half-way wouldn't feel so bad, but I was starting to feel anxious at that point; my breathing was shallower and my heart was racing. The climb felt really difficult; it was very dark and the steps were just as uneven as I remembered. The spiral staircase started to make me feel dizzy and the people in front seemed to be rushing to get to the top. The people behind me had already stopped once to catch their breath, but I pushed on, which I regretted once in the clock tower.

As we stepped into the descent room, the final person from the previous group was hanging over the drop-zone. I made the crucial error of looking down that hole; absolutely terrifying. My head started to spin and I forgot how to breathe. I got my phone out to distract myself, but as others started to dangle their phones over the hole, the abseil instructor told them not to cause a distraction, and there went my photo opportunity. Still, there were more important things on my mind; I had to learn how to actually abseil before going down that death-hole.

There was a very short bit of thick rope attached to one of the walls of the clock tower, right next to a tiny window, which was a screaming reminder of how high up we were. As we took it in turns to be fastened to the wall (practising on the rope), the instructor kept looking at me as if to say "are you OK?" I think my politeness sometimes comes across as fear; letting others go first on the test-rope and listening too intently could come across as not wanting to do it. In reality, I would have loved to have gone first. The ordeal couldn't have been over fast enough.

It was harder than I imagined to hold my own weight and not trap my gloves in the mechanism. With more room (and height) I hoped to find a smoother motion. I guess I would have no other choice when descending. Down was the only option. Before I could worry anymore, the two men standing either side of the drop called out to our group. "Can we have the first one please?"

One woman had to go to work after doing this, so she was happy to go first. I hear that she even did some acrobatics towards the bottom. I'm glad I didn't know that before my own descent. I felt enough pressure just trying to remember how to use my arms, never mind any other parts of my body. Next went a lady who was 'tricked' into this by her daughter; her nerves were starting to show and her descent was very slow, but hats off to her for taking it in her stride. I could see the fear in her face and movements; she wasn't great at following instructions, but she didn't hesitate when it came to jumping off the solid platform.

Then the guy doing it on behalf of his poorly sister stepped up; nobody was going to argue with him, he was the fastest of the lot of us to step off the platform. I felt quite moved seeing what a difference some strong motivation can make.

Then went the mother and daughter combo, the daughter first. She felt very sick and before her turn they had to change some of the Carabiner clips because they were getting too warm, this made her wait seem much longer and also added to her nerves. She seemed to reach the bottom at record-speed though, leaving just me and her mother at the top. Once the daughter had gone, her mother's nerves started to show, I almost felt like hugging her but I often misread these things. I stayed my distance but did a little 'go get 'em!' dance for her as she looked up at me from the drop.

Despite watching 4 other people go down, she also forgot which parts of the rope to hold onto and butterflies started to fill my stomach. The last abseiler was hanging above the opening of the drop with her eyes tightly shut, and I could feel her fear. I just watched her, longing to help her, but also dreading the fact that I was the only person left at the top. I was next.

My body went into complete automatic mode. I took deep breaths and walked towards the two men either side of the drop. I looked straight ahead the whole time; I couldn't tell you what either guy looked like and I certainly couldn't tell you what was happening below me. I went to an entirely different place in my mind, knowing that all of the fear was in the 98 feet below me; a section I had dismissed entirely from my own perception. Stepping off the platform was actually quite comforting; for the first time I felt the harness cradle my body and I felt very secure. As the guys moved my hands into the right position (my gloves were still determined to become trapped in the mechanism) I just kept thinking "please, please hurry up" It was like waiting for your mouth to go numb at the dentist's. You've gone too far to turn back and now you just want to get it over with.

"If you can, remember to enjoy the view" said the instructor, as I hung there in mid-air. "Are you coming down this way?" I asked her, to which she replied "No way, I'm taking the stairs." "Ready?" asked the guy to my left. "Hell yeah." I replied, and I started to loosen my grip. I was slowly moving downwards, quite smoothly and picking up speed, just as if I were sliding down a very thin pole. I knew I would still be too high to not panic if I looked down, so I kept admiring the architecture at my ever-changing eye level. However, this started to make me feel quite travel sick (something I suffer with quite heavily). As I plucked up the courage to turn my eyes downwards, I was met with a reassuring view; I could see the entire cathedral, I could see daylight again and I could see my family to the left-hand-side of the huge crowd below.

My hands remained open for the most part, but I gripped tighter occasionally in an attempt to slow down; to admire the view. I was just so happy to be moving towards the ground.

I could hear the clicks of Rick's camera echo through the entire cathedral and I automatically plastered a smile across my face. Before I knew it, the guy at the bottom of the rope grabbed hold of my foot and helped me to my feet at the bottom. The round of applause made me blush but I didn't care anymore, in the words of Stephen Chbosky; in that moment, I swear I was infinite.

I sense that other heights won't feel so bad now. I'll just have to tell myself "at least I don't have to abseil down this one."

Other things I did that qualify conquering heights:

At one point I leaned dangerously far out of a second-storey window – there was a hedgehog on the concrete below and I practically offered myself as a snack. I also went to the very top of the tallest tower of Lincoln Cathedral with some friends (470 feet above sea-level and 240 feet above ground – that's 44 times my own height.)

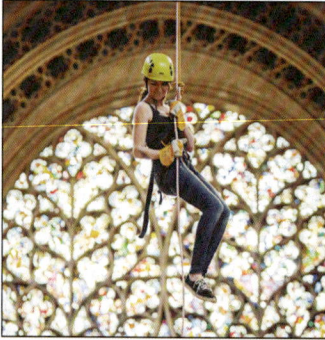

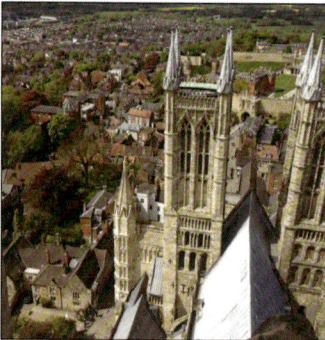

Chapter Eleven:

PUTTING QUESTIONS IN YOUR MOUTH

(as only a newly brave person would)

1. Overall, did you act braver?

To bury my modesty for a second, I was actually quite impressed at how calm I was throughout many of these tasks. In most cases I don't think you'd have particularly noticed my fear if you were unaware of it. This is perhaps with the exception of the flying challenge, where I was deathly silent for almost the entire time (very unlike me). I did find myself saying "yes" to many more opportunities than I would have done before, though. I hope this is a habit that sticks now that the project is over.

2. After everything, do you now feel braver?

It was definitely the flying challenge that turned the tables for me. After that, no challenge seemed like it could be more difficult. In fact, whenever I am struggling with anything, I just say to myself "at least I'm not on a plane right now", which helps a lot. Although that's probably not doing that particular fear any favours. I still put things off that I know will be difficult or potentially painful, but I do also get a reminder of how brave I've been whenever I look down in the shower. Bonus.

3. What fears were next?

Fears eleven to thirteen were 'blood', 'the dark' and 'dogs'. Those three things often go together a lot in our household. I'm quite glad I didn't have to see much blood during these challenges but I would have loved to have been drowned in dogs. Perhaps there's a part-two project idea in there somewhere? Maybe I could get Ross Kemp on board; he's pretty bad-ass.

4. What fears did other people guess could have been in the top ten?

Other people really enjoyed the guessing game, answers ranged from 'sharks' to 'commitment', but I'm surprised some of them didn't appear in the top 10. Some good guesses included things like 'wasps', 'prison', 'becoming disfigured', 'losing your sight' and 'death'.

5. What fears would you add to your own top 10 list?

Losing my memory — this is something I freak out about quite a lot, the possibility of forgetting who I am or who other people are. Moths — I'm not sure why I find them so creepy, I think it's the fact that they're hairy. I don't like bugs in general, treading on snails when it's dark makes me cringe every time. I also have a very real phobia of seeing people vomit. And I dislike being too far from home.

6. Which challenge did you enjoy the most?

Tricky question actually. I loved holding the spider because it was such a relief to find one, and holding mice made me very tempted to buy some as pets. I also enjoyed getting all my friends together and making them dress as clowns. I think I'll go for clowns. It was great to get so many others involved.

7. In which challenge did you surprise yourself the most?

Needles. I had no problem getting my boobs out in front of a stranger, which I fully expected to petrify me. I usually need to know someone at least an hour prior to that.

8. Which was the worst?

Without a shred of doubt; flying. I knew it would be. It's the combination of at least three fears in one: heights, small spaces and crowds. Throw some snakes in there and we've got ourselves a movie. This was closely followed by crowds and public speaking.

9. What was the hardest part of the entire project?

Trying to decide on the challenges was, without a doubt, the hardest part. Everybody has a different opinion on what they deem impressive, though; my mum absolutely hates flying but she'd rather fly than abseil. I wouldn't have guessed that in a million years; abseiling is over with so quickly! I got frustrated when I couldn't get into a more extreme situation for a challenge too, such as holding only one spider, whereas someone with a crippling phobia probably couldn't have even been in the same room as one. I am my own worst critic, I suppose.

10. Would you do this project again?

I'd like to think that I would, but I wouldn't do it any-time soon. It took up a lot more time than I had initially planned, not just when completing the challenges but also planning the dates and travel that was needed for each one. Putting the book together also took a lot of effort and a lot of editing, though the results made it all worthwhile.

11. What's next?

It has been suggested to me that I should turn this project into a live blog, where people could offer their own phobias for me to conquer. I have a feeling, however, that people wouldn't take it very seriously and would ask me to sit in a school assembly naked or something. It would then turn into a race to see who could get me arrested the fastest. So I will probably turn my hand to writing fiction next. ...Probably.

12. How are your nipples?

It's surprising how many friends have asked me this recently. They're wonderful, thank you so much for asking. How are yours?!

13. What did you learn about yourself?

This question might sound corny, but I think it's an important one. Why challenge yourself to do anything in life, if you're not going to grow somehow in the process? I wasn't setting out on a journey to discover the cause of all fear, I simply wanted to push my own limits. It's just a bonus that I've also learned quite a lot in the process.

I became stressed, anxious and impatient just planning the challenges, before even attempting to face the fear itself. In the end, I was really surprised at the strength of my own willpower. I'm pretty good at quitting anything that is out of my comfort zone, so I wasn't sure I'd be able to complete all 10 challenges (especially flying) but my determination wouldn't let me quit.

For the majority of this year, I was constantly looking for a 'better' challenge opportunity. The list of phobias was always at the back of my mind, so much so that it became an obsession. I wanted to be braver than my previous self, even if that was as recent as the week before. If I'd already held a snake last week, I wanted to try and hold 2 this week (or 5!).

I'm the only person (that I can find) who has taken on these 10 fears within such a short space of time, but I hope that some competition arises. It feels good to be braver than the average Brit. I invite you to join me here; in my completely exhausted but incredibly proud, state *collapses off sofa*.

It's been a very interesting year, not just through learning lots about myself, but by also learning a lot about the people around me. Fear is so commonly seen as 'weakness' that it is acknowledged as shameful and often hidden. Yet people are very happy to admit/talk about their own fears if you ask them. This quickly helped me to gain some perspective about how logical my own fears are.

The highlight for me was watching numerous adults cry at the top of an abseil rope (wait for it; I'm not that mean...) and yet; not a single person backed out. Fear was in the room, but we all blatantly chose to ignore it.

Chapter Twelve:

Your phobia isn't that weird...

(what is fear?)

Although suffering from a phobia might make you feel limited, frustrated and sometimes weird as Hell, I hope this chapter helps you come to terms with your anxiety a little bit more.

Experiencing fear is one of the most innate things to our existence; it's nature's defense mechanism. Without fear we would cross roads without looking, walk straight off the edges of buildings and invite people with contagious illnesses to our dinner parties. Those with a heightened sense of fear have continued to breed and survive, creating an army of similarly anxious beings who will continue to multiply (supposing they don't have social anxiety and never find a mate).

Fear is just as relevant today as it was in caveman times, except instead of being attacked for the fresh carcass you've just gone to great lengths to acquire, it's your wallet that the delinquents are after.

If you ever feel like you're overreacting to a sudden noise or shadow, don't be embarrassed; our brains automatically jump to the worst conclusion and then work backwards. This is for our own protection. Before your brain has time to scan its memory bank for previous non-harmful sounds, it assumes you're about to be murdered. In the rare instance that there is, in fact, a killer clown inside your house, your body's totally got your back.

Whenever we pull a terrified face, similar to that of Munch's *The Scream* painting, or accidentally let out a shriek like a peacock in heat, we're actually alerting others to potential danger and saving mankind (these signs are universally understood). Seriously, it's OK to sweat it – even the increase of anxiety-induced moisture is there to warn others about danger. It turns out that humans can subconsciously differentiate the perspiration caused by exercise, and that which is produced by fear; alerting themselves to any potential threat to their safety.

A lot of unusual things happen to our bodies during the sensation of fear, but they all have their reasons. With the sudden release of epinephrine, norepinephrine and dozens of other hormones, our body starts to change in preparation to either run away as fast as we can, or fight whatever we feel threatened by. Our pupils dilate to let in more light, the veins close to the surface of our skin constrict – sending blood to more useful organs (and creating the 'chill' that we often feel), adrenaline tenses up our muscles and our digestion and immune systems shut down to send energy elsewhere. We often become less-focused on small tasks because our brains are distracted by the bigger problem. Most of the time, we can tap into about 65% of the energy in our muscles. When experiencing fear, however, a combination of adrenaline, focus and sheer determination all come together to enable the super-human feats we so often hear about during near-death experiences. Like the ability to hurl a shoe all the way across a room, rather than it stopping, feebly, halfway to its 8-legged destination.

The human brain is made up of different regions which play numerous roles and control a huge variety of different functions. Some regions specialise in complex thought (probably a small region in my case) but the part at the very core of the brain is called 'The Lizard Brain'. This region handles basic body functions like breathing and coordination, but it also controls our most basic survival urges such as feeding, mating and defending ourselves. These instincts have been ingrained in us for tens of thousands of years and although circumstances may change throughout different time periods, our primal urges stay the same. We have very little control over them.

Some of the same genetic material that is found in The Lizard Brain, also exists in both the heart and the gut, so 'gut reactions' and 'heartwarming feelings' are actually quantifiable things. I once went to grab a heavy desk lamp when I heard a noise upstairs – a good gut reaction – I then dropped it on my foot; blinded by the adrenaline rush.

Almost every phobia has a name, from the fear of balloons (globophobia) to fear of sleep (hypnophobia). I struggled to think of something to fear that didn't have a scientific name. Nothing makes you feel less-alone than knowing someone else has suffered before you. Us 'mere mortals' are not the only ones who suffer from slightly illogical fears, either. Here are some celebrities who suffer in unusual ways:

1. Christina Ricci - Plants *(Botanophobia)*

2. Pamela Anderson - Mirrors *(Eisoptrophobia)*

3. Orlando Bloom - Pigs *(Swinophobia)*

4. Matthew McConaughey - Revolving Doors *(Orbitagoraphobia)*

5. Kelly Osbourne - Being touched *(Haphephobia)*

6. Keanu Reeves - The dark *(Nyctophobia)*

7. Oprah Winfrey - Chewing gum *(Chiclephobia)*

8. Robert Pattinson - Horses *(Equinophobia)*

9. Madonna - Thunder *(Brontophobia)*

10. David Beckham - Untidiness *(Ataxophobia)*

Are you feeling better yet? If not, just imagine how clean your house would be if David Beckham moved in.

No matter how debilitating or stressful your fear is, your mind has formed neural pathways which deem it to be logical, and so your body is simply responding. My heart rate increases every time I talk to a stranger, I dread every train journey no matter how short and Matthew McConaughey can't use revolving doors.

We're all pretty weird, really. My advice is to become as famous as you can so that your 'unreasonable' weather, entrance and accommodation demands are met with a less-than-discreet eye-roll, but complete compliance. DON'T YOU KNOW WHO I AM? *touches Kelly Osbourne*

Chapter Thirteen:

JUST FOR THE TRISKAIDEKAPHOBICS

(sorry)

CREDIT

(…where credit's due)

Book reviews (on sleeve):
Gyles Lingwood - Very much my creative guru, thank you for contributing to this madness.

Ash Billinghay - My effeminate creative guru, I owe you a burger or five million.

Illustrations:
Rosie Ablewhite - My sister from the same mister. My wombmate. My real-life clone. Thank you for turning this book into one I can happily judge by it's cover.

Design:
Rick Nunn - You've turned my dream into a reality, thank you so much.

Editing:
John O'Nolan - Thank you for taking on so much (more so than when you first agreed to help with this), but also for letting me live afterwards.

Chapter 1 - Clowns
Yazmin McGill, **Steven Fairley**, **Tom Jacobs**, **Rosie Ablewhite**, **Robyn Jenner**, **Amy Lincoln**, **Sean Jones**, **Kris Nielsen**, **Moya Nielsen**, **Helen McCarron**, **Lyndsey Kemsley**, **Suzannah Turner** and **Ralph Fairley** - Clowns

Rick Nunn - Photographer

Thank you for the best evening of the entire year.

Chapter 2 - Crowds
Rick Nunn - Leeds Fest Buddy/Gro-Pro Handler/ Dancer.

Chapter 3 - Flying
Rick Nunn - Flight buddy (ILY).

Chapter 4 - Needles
Rosie Ablewhite - Coffee Bringer/Home Carrier

Eternal Angel, Lincoln - Piercing Studio. Absolutely brilliant people.

Chapter 5 - Mice
Rick Nunn - Mouse-holding Buddy

White Post Farm, Farnsfield - Location

Chapter 6 - Small spaces
Di Ablewhite - Car Boot Owner. Thanks for the tiny car, bitch.

Rick Nunn - Go-Pro Supplier/Live-feed set-up

Bandit Nunn-Whittaker - Post-trauma Cuddler

Chapter 7 - Spiders
Spider-man - Spider Provider

Fanny (The Chilean Rose Babe) - Spider

Rick Nunn - Spider Buddy/Photographer

Chapter 8 - Public Speaking
Heather Bennett - Bride

Dean Bennett - Groom

Eleanor Ball - Speech Buddy, Co-Speech-Writer/Dance Partner/Drink Buddy)

Rick Nunn - Photographer

Eric Ho - Praiseworthy Public Speaker

Chapter 9 - Snakes
Rosie Ablewhite - Snake-holding Buddy 1/Photographer

Robyn Jenner - 2nd Snake-holding Buddy

Woodside Wildlife & Falconry Park, Lincoln - Location

L.A Reptiles, Lincoln - Better Location

Chapter 10 - Heights
Lincoln Cathedral, Lincoln - Venue

Nottingham Hospitals Charity - Organisers

Rick Nunn - Photographer

Rosie Ablewhite - Support Network

Profit:
Andy Farrell - Charity Chooser

The **bone & soft tissue cancer** charity

Sarcoma UK - http://sarcoma.org.uk

If you have purchased this book (or donated in any way) then you are helping a very, very worthy cause. Sarcoma is a rare type of cancer which means the charity is lesser known. Your time and money leads to life-changing research and every person makes a difference.

Thank you for being one of them.